Raise Creative Thinkers

A Guide to Developing Children's Creative Intelligence

Jackie McCarthy

Illustrated by: Alexandra Lore McCarthy
Additional Drawings by: Brady and Bailey McCarthy

For information about this title, to order other books and/or electronic media, as well as accompanying products, or to inquire about speaker workshops, contact the publisher:

Raise Creative Kidz
http://RaiseCreative Kidz.com
www.facebook.com/RaiseCreativeKidz
Jackie@RaiseCreativeKidz.com

ISBN: 978-0-9907840-0-5

Printed in the United States of America

Cover and Interior design: 1106 Design

I dedicate this book to my three incredible and very creative children — Brady, Bailey, and Alexandra. You inspire me to be a better parent, a better person, and to do what I can to make this a better world for you to live and grow in. Every day, living with the three of you is like jumping into a *Mary Poppins*-inspired, water-colored painting and riding a carousel of race horses.

To my very supportive husband, Kevin: Thank you for allowing me to pursue all my crazy, creative ideas. None of this would be possible without you.

To my sister, Mary, who has always been one of my biggest fans — no matter what project I am working on. Thank you for believing in me enough for me to believe in myself.

And, to my parents, for understanding the importance of kids developing creativity in their own back yard and for raising the seven of us to know how to use our imagination to turn a box, a bed sheet, and an empty paper-towel roll into magic.

Table of Contents

Chapter One
Creativity Crisis

When I was growing up, forty years ago, Magna Doodle was one of the top kids' toys. The laptop hadn't been invented yet. The very first mobile phones had just come out, and they looked more like a *Get Smart* shoe phone than the sleek models they have today. There were fewer than ten TV channels and "Pong," a two-dimensional, black-and-white video game consisting of two straight lines and a white dot, where you would hit the "ball" across the screen to each other, a.k.a. ping pong, was all the rage. Needless to say, a kid's own imagination didn't have all that much competition from technology back then.

FAST FORWARD TO TODAY...

The average ten-year-olds have their own cell phones, which are fully decked out with all sorts of game and social media apps; most households have at least one high-resolution gaming console attached to one of the home's numerous TVs; computers/laptops/tablets are commonly owned in multiples by most every family member; and there are so many TV channels that you need an electronic guide to help you keep track of them all. Add this explosion of technology to the heightened academic pressures in schools, for kids to just memorize facts, and it's no surprise that we find that our children's creativity scores are in a free-fall.

Recent research shows that there is a Creativity Crisis in this country. The measure of creativity, like the measure of intelligence, used to show an increase with each generation, but, in 1990, that trend reversed. In 2010, Kyung Hee Kim at the College of William & Mary shared the results of her study of 300,000 *Torrance Tests of Creative Thinking* scores of children and adults.

Kim found that, since 1990, creativity scores have consistently and significantly gone down. The study found that children are becoming:

- less verbally or emotionally expressive
- less empathetic
- less humorous
- less imaginative
- less able to visualize ideas
- less able to see things from different angles
- less able to fantasize
- less able to be future-oriented

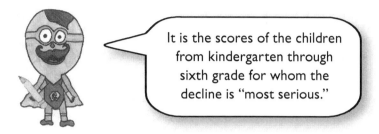

It is the scores of the children from kindergarten through sixth grade for whom the decline is "most serious."

The likely culprits in this decline, not surprisingly, are time spent in front of the TV and playing video games, as well as the increasing academic curriculum standards in school, leaving little to no room in the day for creativity.

The good news is that, as parents, there is much we can do to start to turn this Creativity Crisis around. All children are born with some degree of creativity. When parents become educated about creativity, they can help their children preserve their natural inclination to it. Research has shown that creativity can be nourished and taught and that creativity training can have a strong effect. Real improvement doesn't happen overnight, but when creativity is fostered through a child's everyday home life, creative brain function improves.

As one of seven children, I grew up in a household that valued creativity. My creative upbringing molded my future occupational role as a marketing executive for a company in the top tier of the Fortune 500. And, when I had my children, I focused my creative inclinations on providing a stimulating home environment of wonder and imagination for them.

It was easy to nurture their innate creativity when they were toddlers and in preschool, but as they entered grade school and middle school, I found myself having to work harder at getting them to focus on creative activities, as I had to compete with homework time, sports practice, and the never-ending pull of the video game. So, when I saw Kyung Hee Kim's research on the decline of our children's ability to be creative—it didn't surprise me. I could see how easily time for working on creative thinking skills could fall by the wayside when there were so many other things to take up my children's time. What it did, though, was to reinvigorate my desire to ensure that my children had ways to work on their Creative Intelligence. I wasn't willing to let such a crucial, life skill-set evaporate for my kids.

I started gathering research on all the benefits of helping children develop their Creative Intelligence. I discovered that the process I had used in my prior occupation as a marketing executive, of taking social and psychological research and turning my findings into creative, actionable ideas, worked equally as well in this domain. So, I started posting my research findings and documenting the creative-thinking skill activities that I was designing for my children on a website that I created, RaiseCreativeKidz. com. This website is dedicated to helping other parents raise more creative thinkers and is the basis for this book.

Use this book as a guide to help educate yourself on what creativity is, how it works, why it's an important skill-set to have, what motivates creative thinking and what hinders it, and what you can do as a parent to help encourage the creative thought process in your own children. The final section is devoted to actionable, hands-on activities you can use with your children to put all this information into action. According to Kyung Hee Kim, "The Creativity Crisis is not an event, but an era of continued decline in most measures of creativity. Reversing this trend will be a process that will require patience and perseverance."

As parents, we each need to take our part in helping to turn this Creativity Crisis around, while helping our children develop a skill that will benefit them greatly throughout their lives.

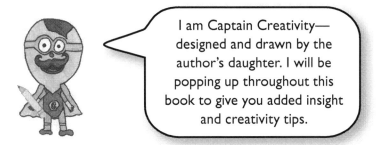

I am Captain Creativity—designed and drawn by the author's daughter. I will be popping up throughout this book to give you added insight and creativity tips.

NOTE: In between each chapter, I have included an example of an *Incomplete Picture Activity* that my children have completed. In this activity, I gave my children a blank piece of paper with only a partial shape drawn on it (e.g., a squiggly line, an open-ended triangle). I asked them to use this partial shape as part of an imaginative drawing. Below each drawing, I share some of my favorite, famous quotes about creativity.

"Be brave enough to live creatively. The creative place is where no one else has been. You have to leave the city of your comfort and go into the wilderness of your intuition. You can't get there by bus, only by hard work and risk and by not quite knowing what you're doing, but what you'll discover will be wonderful. What you'll discover will be yourself."

— Alan Alda, Commencement Speech at Connecticut College, 1980 (actor, director, and screenwriter)

Chapter Two

What Is Creativity?

CREATIVITY IS NOT EXCLUSIVE TO THE ARTS

Although creativity is often associated with "creative" subjects, such as art and music, creativity is not subject specific. A person, for example, can be creative in science, math, technology or even cooking. Creative thought appears in almost all aspects of life: From the way kids solve conflicts on the playground, to the way a child negotiates a later bedtime, to how a scientist comes up with a new discovery, to the development of an innovative product. Creativity is displayed in some by their talent in the arts, but in others it can be seen in their ability to generate a number of different, unique ideas in various subject matters.

Finding a new way to help customers, designing a unique app for the smart phone, or developing a new use for a common household item all show creativity.

CREATIVITY IS CONNECTING PIECES OF KNOWLEDGE IN A UNIQUE WAY

All creativity is based on knowledge and experiences one has accumulated in certain areas. Creativity is just finding an unusual way to connect those pieces of knowledge that already exist for a person.

According to Steve Jobs, co-founder of Apple Inc., "Creativity is just connecting things. When you ask creative people how they did something, they feel a little guilty because they didn't really do it; they just saw something. It seemed obvious to them after a while. That's because they were able to connect experiences they've had and synthesize new things."

You can't be creative in an area that you don't have any previous knowledge in, but you can use others' knowledge in a particular area to enhance your own. Thomas Edison filled notebooks on new ideas others had published that he found interesting. It didn't matter what field it was in. He felt any good idea, whether it worked or not in its current form, could perhaps spark a new idea in him. To Edison, an idea needed to be original only in how he could adapt it to a problem that he was working on.

CREATIVITY IS NOT JUST THE BIG IDEAS

We can all point out the big creative ideas — Michelangelo's painting of the Sistine Chapel ceiling, Steve Jobs' invention of the iPhone, Jonas Salk's discovery of the Polio vaccine — but creativity is not just the big ideas. There have been many creative geniuses that have made history. But, there are far more everyday acts of creativity by ordinary people. Everything around us — the conveniences in our homes, traffic flow in our cities, home grown inventions sold on infomercials, new smart phones/cars/TVs — are conceived and developed by everyday people who implement creative ideas.

Creativity is not simply about coming up with big ideas, but coming up with practical solutions to everyday problems and then applying them to real-life situations.

Kids show everyday creativity through a fifth-grader's science fair project, a high-school student's innovative hair style, a scrapbook they put together, the excuses they formulate for not having finished their homework, the way they might decorate their room, a creative idea they come up with to raise money for a school or community project, or it might be seen in the essay they write for their college application. While some students fit into more traditional creative slots, such as artist or musician, many others express themselves through more everyday acts.

ANYONE CAN BE CREATIVE

For many years, it was believed human creativity was inherited. We have finally come to believe that everyone has some level of creativity and that the environment, especially childhood experiences, plays a significant role in how creativity develops for each individual.

Boston College Professor John Dacey conducted a study[1] of 100 New England adolescents and found that creative people's family lives differ from those of people with ordinary ability. "The parents of creative children tend to be more nurturing and less discipline focused," Dacey said, "and humor is often a hallmark of their family lives."

Though all individuals can be creative, different combinations of abilities, personality traits, and home experiences make them more or less able to express their creative potential. Some children will miss the opportunity to develop their creativity without encouragement and support in school or in the home, as shown by the longitudinal study completed by Land and Jarmen in 1992.

In the Land study, 1,600 three-to-five-year-old kids were given a creativity test. Ninety-eight percent of those kids tested scored at a level they called creative "genius" for divergent thinking. When the very same kids were tested five years later (ages 8–10), only 32 percent scored in this top tier. After another five years (ages 13–15), only 10 percent of the same kids scored in the top tier. By 1992, 200,000 twenty-five-year-olds had taken the same battery of tests, and only 2 percent had scored in the top level. Land believed one of the reasons for this decline was that education is driven by the idea of "one correct answer" and thereby stifles the act of imagining many different ideas, which is what creativity is based on.

www.RaiseCreativeKidz.com   Title: **Birds**

Alexx

"The creative person wants to be a know-it-all. He wants to know about all kinds of things — ancient history, nineteenth-century mathematics, current manufacturing techniques, hog futures. Because he never knows when these ideas might come together to form a new idea. It may happen six minutes later, or six months, or six years. But, he has faith that it will happen."

> — Carl Ally (an American advertising executive who was inducted into the American Advertising Federation Hall of Fame).

Chapter Three

Why Is Creativity Important?

Educators and parents see that the demand for creativity and creative thinking for solving complex problems and driving future economies is growing, yet, according to research, students are less prepared to lead the innovation of tomorrow. Developing one's creativity is a crucial factor in being able to compete in this fast-changing world. It can have an effect on our children in a variety of areas.

SOCIAL, EMOTIONAL, AND PHYSICAL WELL-BEING

The importance of creativity is often greatly underestimated. Being able to come up with new ideas and solve everyday problems plays a critically important role in learning and personal development, as well as building self-esteem. Learning to creatively problem solve, also helps children to:

- develop initiative and creativity
- enhance their manipulative skills and mathematical thinking
- gain confidence in their ability to work things out for themselves
- increase their social leadership skills

According to Edward de Bono, one of the leading authorities in creative thinking, "Creativity is a great motivator because it makes people interested in what they are doing. [It] gives hope that there can be a worthwhile idea. Creativity makes life more fun and more interesting."

Creativity can affect physical well-being as well. It has been found to decrease mortality risk and predict a longer life.[2] Creative thinking seems to reduce stress and keep the brain healthy. Other studies have linked this trait with lower metabolic risk, higher self-rated health, and more appropriate stress response. One possible reason creativity is protective of health is because it draws on a variety of neural networks within the brain. This study's author, Nicholas Turiano, states, "Individuals high in creativity maintain the integrity of their neural networks even into old age."

Turiano also cites creative people's ability to handle stress — they tend not to get as easily flustered when faced with an emotional or physical hurdle. Stress is known to harm overall health, including cardiovascular, immune, and cognitive systems. "Creative people may see stressors more as challenges that they can work to overcome rather than as stressful obstacles they can't overcome," Turiano says. The results suggest that practicing creative-thinking techniques could improve anyone's health by lowering stress and exercising the brain.

Our society is characterized by uncertainty and rapid change. For our children, nothing is more important than learning to think creatively — learning to come up with innovative solutions to unexpected situations that will inevitably arise throughout their lives.

FUTURE INNOVATION

Facts and figures can take you only so far if you can't "think outside the box" and imagine different ways in which to use that information. Innovation comes from our imagination, our ability to picture things that don't currently exist in reality.

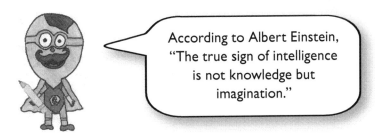

According to Albert Einstein, "The true sign of intelligence is not knowledge but imagination."

Steve Jobs didn't mention apps, media, or even a touchscreen when he asked his engineering team to come up with the original idea for the iPhone. Instead, his mandate, according to former iPhone product marketing manager Bob Borchers, was simple. "Create the first phone that people would fall in love with. That's what he told us," Borchers said. How do you define what will make people fall in love with a phone? Well, you need to use your creative imagination.

Sir Ken Robinson, a creativity consultant for many Fortune 500 companies, reports that CEOs are always saying, "We need people who can be innovative, who can think differently." He states, "If you look at the mortality rate among companies, it's massive. America is now facing the biggest challenge it's ever faced — to maintain its position in the world economies. All these things demand high levels of innovation, creativity, and ingenuity. At the moment, instead of promoting creativity, I think we're systematically educating it out of our kids."

BUSINESS SUCCESS IN A COMPETITIVE GLOBAL ENVIRONMENT

As schools and parents have gotten more and more focused on academic achievement and after-school activities, we have also been losing sight of the one characteristic most corporations have come to value the most: Creativity. According to a 2010 study by IBM, CEOs state that creativity is now the most important leadership quality for success in business.[3]

In a recent conversation with the *Boston Globe*, Shelley Carson, who has a PhD in psychology from Harvard University, states: "In the business world, creativity is now the number-one quality that headhunters are looking for in top-level chief executives. Most of the elite business schools in the country now have courses on creativity, and many Fortune 500 companies have hired creativity consultants." The ability to think creatively, to come up with novel solutions and ideas, will be of the utmost importance for an individual to be able to succeed in such a competitive, global environment.

A FAST-CHANGING WORLD

"Understanding, identifying, and nurturing the creative potential is relevant in education if we want students to be able to solve academic and personal problems and challenges, to find innovative solutions and alternatives, and to have better tools and resources for success in a fast-changing world," Dr. Rosa Aurora Chávez-Eakle, MD, PhD, of the Maryland State Department of Education Council for Gifted and Talented, states in a recent research paper.[4] She goes on to say, "Creative Thinking not only enhances our ability to adapt to our environment and circumstances, but also allows us to transform those environments and circumstances. Creativity has been identified as a key component for survival and resilience. If we want to teach children to become productive human beings and be more satisfied with what they do with their lives, we need to support them in the process of discovering and enjoying their creative potential."

In a recent TED talk, Sir Ken Robinson, of the British government's advisory committee on creative and cultural education, stated that "the challenges we currently face are without precedent. More people live on this planet now than at any other time in history. The world's population has doubled in the past thirty years. We're facing an increasing strain on the world's natural resources. Technology is advancing at a headlong rate of speed. It's transforming how people work, think, and connect. It's transforming our cultural values. We are facing unprecedented strains on our political and financial institutions, on health care, and on education, and we're going to need every ounce of ingenuity, imagination, and creativity to confront these problems."

"If you look at the magnitude, the complexity of issues and problems facing society, there is no question that we need creative thinking. The ability to produce new knowledge, rather than learn and use existing knowledge, will be our most cherished trait." (Prof. John Dacey)

The Director for the *Torrance Center of Creativity*, Bonnie Cramond, believes "If creativity goes undeveloped in our children, society may lose such important contributions as the ideas from unwritten novels, medical breakthroughs, economic prosperity from new business ventures, beautiful art and music, proclamations for social change, and resource-saving inventions." As our world becomes more complex and problems become more challenging, the need for creative individuals to address these situations in innovative ways increases.

"A man may die, nations may rise and fall, but an idea lives on."

— John F. Kennedy (former President of the United States)

Chapter Four

Can Creativity Be Taught?

R oger von Oech, in his book *A Whack on the Side of the Head*, recounts a teacher's exercise in examining creativity. The teacher drew a dot on the chalkboard and asked a class of sophomores to identify it. They responded with the obvious: A chalk dot. The day before, she had asked a group of kinder-gartners, and they had come up with numerous examples of what it might be: The top of a telephone pole, a squashed bug, an owl's eye, a cigar butt, a rotten egg, and so on. Somewhere between childhood and adulthood, many of us lose the ability to be creative and the instinct to search for more than one right answer. The Land study (1992) that I referred to earlier showed the same pattern, with 98 percent of kindergartners showing creative "genius" levels in divergent thinking, that level dropping to 32 percent by 4th grade, and only 10 percent scoring on the creative genius level by eighth grade.

So, what can we do to help our children cultivate creativity? Every brain has the potential to be creative. All brains have a great ability to continually change and develop. Research has shown that, although it may not make an Einstein out of everyone, practice and exercise can definitely make any brain more creative. "It is an undervalued skill that anyone can cultivate."[5]

Since research shows that people start off more creative in childhood and lose much of their creative ability along the way, replacing it with conformity, it tends to follow that our job as parents is more to keep that inherent creativity alive in our children and nurture it over the years, instead of having to teach our children creativity from scratch. The essence of creativity is already there, but it can be improved and kept stimulated by providing our children with the right exercises, knowledge, experiences, and environment. Children's creativity may be getting stifled in school and in society, but, at least at home, you can be nourishing and stimulating it. You want to help your child keep that part of the brain active that is responsible for generating multiple ideas and solutions instead of letting it move toward society's idea of "one right answer" and functional fixedness.

Psychologist Abraham Maslow said, "The key question isn't 'What fosters creativity?' But, it is 'Why in God's name isn't everyone creative? Where was the human potential lost? How was it crippled?' I think, therefore, a good question might be 'Why do people not create or innovate?' We have to abandon that sense of amazement in the face of creativity, as if it was a miracle if anybody created anything."

A US study of 1,000 college-educated professionals[6] sheds new light on the role of creativity in career success and the growing belief that creativity is not just a personality trait, but a learned skill. Based on the study, 85 percent of respondents agree creative thinking is critical for problem solving in their career, and 68 percent of respondents believe creativity is a skill that can be learned. Nearly three-quarters (71 percent) say creative thinking should be "taught as a class — like math or science." Seventy-eight percent of respondents said they wished they had more creative ability, which they defined as "thinking out of the box" or "the ability to come up with innovative ideas." Eighty-two percent wished they'd had more exposure to creative thinking as students.

Fast Company, the world's leading progressive business magazine, found in a recent poll of their list of the *Most Creative People in Business*, that 73 percent believed creativity can be learned, with many citing the importance of being open to new experiences and unfamiliar ways of thinking. More than a quarter of these creative respondents credited their parents for focusing their creative abilities.

"Creativity is merely a plus name for regular activity. Any activity becomes creative when the doer cares about doing it right, or better."

— John Updike (a Pulitzer Prize-winning author)

Chapter Five

Barriers to Creativity

There appear to be two main barriers that have caused such a decline in the creativity development in children over the past two-dozen years. They are the increasing academic curriculum standards in school and the huge increase in time children are spending in front of the TV and computer, as well as playing video games. The numbers speak for themselves.

EDUCATION

According to Mitchel Resnick, in a paper he wrote for the MIT Media Lab,[7] the increase in academic curriculum standards is starting as early as kindergarten. Resnick feels that the "traditional kindergarten approach to learning — characterized by a spiraling cycle of Imagine, Create, Play, Share, Reflect, and back to Imagine — is ideally suited to the needs of the 21st century, helping learners develop the creative-thinking skills that are critical to success and satisfaction in today's society."

However, in his view, "kindergarten is undergoing a dramatic change. For nearly 200 years, since the first kindergarten opened in 1837, kindergarten has been a time for telling stories, building castles, drawing pictures, and learning to share. But, that has started to change. Today, more and more kindergarten children are spending time filling out phonics worksheets and memorizing math flashcards. In short, kindergarten is becoming more like the rest of school." Resnick believes "exactly the opposite is needed: Instead of making kindergarten like the rest of school, we need to make the rest of school (indeed, the rest of life) more like kindergarten."

But, formal education is getting further away and not closer to nurturing creativity. In a recent survey,[8] 89 percent of educators and 87 percent of parents agreed that teachers could be doing more to teach creativity, but they believe that there are barriers in the way of that change.

- Teachers (86 percent) agreed that there needs to be "transformation in the way schools work" in order to foster creativity.
- They also agreed (85 percent) that, in order to teach creativity, educators must be given more tools and techniques.

The survey identified several barriers that both teachers and parents agreed stood in the way of creativity in schools. Those barriers included:

- Schools do not allow enough time for creativity
- Creativity is not valued by the education system

- Schools do not have the tools required to effectively foster creativity in education
- Creativity is not something that can be assessed under the current education system

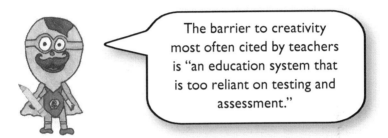

The barrier to creativity most often cited by teachers is "an education system that is too reliant on testing and assessment."

The survey also asked respondents for the single most important step that must be taken to promote and foster creativity in the classroom. The top five suggestions from teachers and parents in the United States were:

1. Provide tools and techniques for educators to teach creativity.

2. Make creativity integral to the curriculum.

3. Reduce mandates that hinder creativity.

4. Improve the curriculum.

5. Reward educators who inspire students to be creative.

"Currently, as students move from K-5 to grades 6–12 and on to higher education, creativity is increasingly treated as a specialized skill," Tracy Trowbridge, worldwide manager of education programs at Adobe, said.

Among American educators surveyed, most (54 percent) indicated that the role of creativity in education has changed in the last twenty-five years, and a larger majority (68 percent) said the role of creativity will be greater in education in the next twenty-five years — yet there is much that needs to change. While we need to keep pushing our schools and government to give creativity the focus it deserves in the education system, as parents, it's important that we are, at least, actively nurturing creativity development at home.

SCREEN TIME

With so much advancement in technology having happened so quickly in these past two decades, it's not surprising that we haven't been able to stay on top of the social ramifications of it all. Did you know that if you add up the average of all the screen time kids spend a day, it would be the equivalent of 114 full days a year watching a screen for fun? According to a survey done by the Kaiser Family Foundation,[9] kids ages 8–18 now spend, on average, an incredible 7½ hours in front of a screen for entertainment each day, 4½ of which are spent watching TV. "For every hour spent watching TV," says University of Texas professor Elizabeth Vandewater, "overall time on creative activities like fantasy play and art projects drops by as much as 11 percent." It's time we took a step back, at least as parents, and tried to sort out how to keep the benefits technology has provided for our children while cutting back on its detriments.

"Passion is one great force that unleashes creativity, because if you're passionate about something, then you're more willing to take risks."

— Yo-Yo Ma (a famous French and American cellist)

Chapter Six
Creativity Crushers

It's not just outside time-constraints that get in the way of our children being able to think creatively. Imaginary mental blocks are constantly getting in the way of their natural, creative abilities as well. Therefore, we must find ways to help our children avoid them. I call these our "Creativity Crushers."

EVALUATION

For some children, the expectation of being evaluated is all that's needed to dampen their creativity. Psychologist Teresa Amabile, a Harvard University professor, conducted an experiment where she asked children to produce a creative product, such as a collage or a short story.[10] She told some of the children that their work would be evaluated for creativity by a panel of experts and that the most creative products would win a prize. Other participants weren't told anything about an evaluation. The results of the experiment showed that the participants who made the most creative products were those who did not know their products would be evaluated. They were the ones just playing, not concerned about whether what they were creating would be considered good or not by someone else.

LOOKING FOR THE "RIGHT ANSWER"

Formal education is always trying to get children to focus on the "correct answer" to the question or problem. To be a good creative thinker, you need to believe that there could be more than one right answer. By coming up with many solutions, one can then have the opportunity to find the best answer instead of just the most obvious answer.

The reason that it is difficult not to fall into the "right answer" pattern is because our brains are highly efficient machines. When a thought process is repeated over and over again, eventually our brain sees a pattern and needs only a bit of information to come up with the end result. Read the paragraph below and decide whether you are determining what you are seeing or if your brain is deciding what you should see.

"Aoccdrnig to rscheearch at Cmabridge Uinvervtisy, it deosn't mttaer in waht oredr the litteers in a wrod are, the olny iprmoetnt tihng is taht the frist and lsat ltteer be at the rghit pclae. The rset can be a ttoal mses and you can sitll raed it wouthit a porbelm. Tihs is besauae ocne we laren how to raed we bgien to aargnre the lteerts in our mnid to see waht we epxcet to see. The huamn mnid deos not raed ervey lteter by istlef, but preecsievs the wrod as a wlohe. We do tihs ucnsoniuscoly wuithot tuhoght." (Graham Rawlinson, a specialist in child development, 1999).

Were you able to read what the note said even though the letters were jumbled? This is because the mind automatically corrects and completes the information to select and activate a pattern. This is why it isn't easy to come up with new ideas. The brain's first reaction is to make the same-old connections and produce the same old ideas over and over again.

Creativity occurs when we reject old, obvious patterns and seek out new information to make new connections. Believing that there can be more than one right answer can lead to new insights, original ideas, and solutions.

FUNCTIONAL FIXEDNESS

People are often very limited in the ways they think about objects, concepts, and people. When something is thought of only in terms of its functionality, then the person is demonstrating "functional fixedness". This is when a person sees only the obvious, the most familiar way, of looking at a problem. This type of thinking often inhibits the problem-solving process because it is narrow in scope.

If naval engineer Richard James had demonstrated functional fixedness, then the popular toy, the Slinky, would never have been invented. In 1943, Mr. James was trying to develop a spring that would support and stabilize sensitive equipment on ships. When one of the springs accidentally fell off a shelf, it continued moving, and James got the idea for a toy. His wife, Betty, came up with the name, and when the Slinky made its debut in late 1945, James sold 400 of the bouncy toys in 90 minutes. Today, more than 250 million Slinkys have been sold worldwide.

FEAR OF FAILURE

Stress and the fear of failure can get in the way of children opening their minds to free thought. We hate being wrong, and yet mistakes often teach us the most. When an experiment failed, Thomas Edison would record what he learned from it. He was very talented in his ability to take an idea that hadn't worked for one problem and to use it successfully to solve another. He never felt like he had failed at something, he always viewed it as just having discovered thousands of things that didn't work.

In a recently published article,[11] we are shown how many creative geniuses had to go through adversity before they were successful and that we need to teach our children that they shouldn't let themselves get discouraged either when confronted by failure. "Albert Einstein was expelled from school because his attitude had a negative effect on serious students. He failed his university entrance exam and had to attend a trade school for one year before finally being admitted. He was the only one in his graduating class who did not get a teaching position because no professor would recommend him. One professor said Einstein was 'the laziest dog' the university ever had. Beethoven's parents were told he was too stupid to be a music composer. Charles Darwin's colleagues called him a fool and what he was doing 'fool's experiments' when he worked on his theory of biological evolution. Walt Disney was fired from his first job on a newspaper because 'he lacked imagination.' Thomas Edison had only two years of formal schooling, was totally deaf in one ear and hard of hearing in the other, was fired from his first job as a newsboy, and later fired from his job as a telegrapher. Still, he became the most famous inventor in the history of the US."

The people who are OK with the idea of failure are the ones who are more likely to be persistent enough to reach a breakthrough. At IDEO, an innovative design firm in Silicon Valley, they have a motto, "Fail often in order to succeed sooner."

DON'T BELIEVE THEY ARE CREATIVE

If children are told they are not creative or tell themselves that, it becomes true. The long-term consequences of labeling children are profound — whether they are labeled positively or negatively. "In a classic study, Robert Rosenthal and Lenore Jacobson told teachers at an elementary school that some of their students had scored in the top 20 percent of a test designed to identify 'academic bloomers' — students who were expected to enter a period of intense, intellectual development over the following year. In fact, the students were selected randomly, and they performed no differently from their unselected peers on a genuine, academic test. A year after convincing the teachers that some of their students were due to bloom, Rosenthal and Jacobson returned to the school and administered the same test. The results were astonishing among the younger children: The 'bloomers', who were no different from their peers a year ago, now outperformed their unselected peers by ten to fifteen IQ points. The teachers fostered the intellectual development of the bloomers, producing a self-fulfilling prophecy in which the students who were baselessly expected to bloom actually outperformed their peers."[12] This is called The *Pygmalion Effect*.

The opposite of The Pygmalion Effect is The Golem Effect. The *Golem Effect* is a psychological phenomenon in which lower expectations placed upon individuals by parents, teachers or the individuals themselves lead to poorer performance by the individuals. This is what happens to children who don't believe they are creative: They stop thinking creatively — it's a self-fulfilling prophecy.

"The secret to creativity is knowing how to hide your sources."

— Albert Einstein

Chapter Seven

Nurturing Creativity at Home

Prominent creativity researcher, E. Paul Torrance, discovered way back in 1965 one important factor that has been shown to influence creativity—that of the family and the family environment. Torrance stated that if children are to develop creatively, then parents must value those personality characteristics that will allow their creative potential to develop. Torrance pointed out that one may have all the internal resources to think creatively, but if the environmental support is lacking than this creativity might never be displayed.

Over the last four decades, much research has been done on varying parenting styles (Baumrind 1967, Berk 2009, Crain 2000). Through this research, four different parenting styles have emerged: Authoritative, Authoritarian, Permissive, and Indifferent.

Authoritative parenting is characterized by parents who hold high expectations and set clear guidelines but are also responsive and nurturing to their children.

Authoritarian parenting is characterized by strict rules, harsh punishments, and little warmth. These parents have high expectations of their children, have very strict rules that they expect to be followed unconditionally, and emphasize discipline over nurturing.

Permissive parenting is sometimes known as indulgent parenting. Parents who exhibit this style make relatively few demands upon their children. Permissive parents are very accepting but exhibit less control over their children and rarely discipline them.

Indifferent parenting is characterized by parents who have little interest or involvement in their children's lives.

Lim and Smith (2008) found that higher levels of acceptance by parents, as seen in both authoritative and permissive parenting styles, are associated with higher levels of creativity in children.[13]

Responsive parenting is the use of warm and accepting behaviors to respond to children's needs and signals. This type of parenting is critically important to young children's development: When parents use these behaviors, a child experiences acceptance of his or her uniqueness. In turn, this encourages a child to continue to communicate his or her needs and interests and to engage in learning interactions. The support associated with responsiveness helps children internalize what they learn in interactions with their caregivers and generalize it to new experiences.

There are a number of things we can do as parents to enhance our children's creative ability. In the list below, check off the areas that you feel you would like to work on doing more of.

☐ Express warmth and nurturance — be responsive and nonjudgmental to your children's ideas and thoughts.

☐ Listen to your children; create a comfortable environment for questions and open discussions — curiosity breeds creativity.

☐ Encourage your children to explore and discuss options and choices — children who are given choices show more creativity than do children who have all choices made for them.

☐ Allow your children to express opinions.

☐ Let them know it's OK to fail — teach them to be non-judgmental of themselves. A brain will censor itself if it comes to learn that getting a wrong answer is a bad thing. Help your child get their brain used to the feeling that is associated with generating a new idea, especially the ambiguity of whether it will work or fail.

☐ Teach them to be persistent and determined without getting themselves frustrated. Don't jump in to fix a problem for them that they don't solve right away. Let them work it out. Show them they can leave a problem and come back to it.

☐ Allow them free thought during play. Encourage them to come up with their own ideas. Don't always provide them the direction or have them play with toys with only one particular function.

☐ Resist perfectionism. Don't take over a child's project because you can do it better or faster. Likewise, resist putting finishing touches on a child's project to make it perfect.

☐ Provide creative activities — children need stimulation and creative problems to solve.

☐ Ensure time for play and fantasy — dramatic play just prior to engaging in problem-solving tasks can lead to more creative thought.

☐ Design a creative environment — physical environments designed to stimulate the senses can enhance creative problem solving. An environment that provides both novelty and variety will greatly aid creativity.

☐ Expose them to a diverse community — give children the opportunity to see and experience other cultures and ways of living. They will be more likely to find an unusual solution to a problem when they have been exposed to more experiences — art, travel, books.

On occasion, look back at this list and make sure you are remembering to incorporate these parenting tips.

As parents, you play an important role in nurturing your children's creativity. You need to allow them the freedom to express themselves and explore their world. Sometimes, it may seem easier and faster to jump in and solve the problem for your children, but stepping in too early can give them the message that you're not confident they can think problems through by themselves. Instead of intervening right away, step back and give them the experience of finding a solution for themselves.

www.RaiseCreativeKidz.com   Title: Good morning, Red Bird

Bailey

"Clean out a corner of your mind and creativity will instantly fill it."

— Dee Hock (Founder and former CEO of the
Visa credit card association)

Chapter Eight

Inspiring Creative Confidence in Our Children

According to the inventor of Mind Mapping, Tony Buzan, *no* individual is *not* creative. He states, "We have a million, million brain cells, and they all integrate. Now anybody with a piece of equipment like that who says, 'I'm not creative' is obviously making a mistake. What has happened is they have not been taught how to use that phenomenal piece of equipment."

David Kelley, the founder of the global design firm, IDEO, which has created thousands of breakthrough inventions, including the first computer mouse for Apple and the stand-up toothpaste tube, states, "I really know that everybody's creative. At IDEO, we take people who, at some point in their childhood, have opted out of being creative, and said 'You know, I'm just not the creative type,' bring them in, and we hold their hand; they have those series of small successes, and, at one point, you see them flip and they say, 'Oh my god, I'm a creative person.' That's the candy for me, so, for the rest of my life, I want to flip as many people as possible. Flip them into self-confidence about creativity. Think about a world where people are walking around thinking of themselves as creative, and they're trying new things all the time."

Kelley believes, "Once you think of yourself as a creative person, you make better decisions...It's just so empowering." He wants to help people regain the creative confidence they lost along the way.

Most everyone is born with some degree of creativeness. Just remember what you used to be like back in kindergarten — with your imaginary play and the drawings you would create. But, as we've discussed in this book, over time, because of social conformity and the rigidness of schools, a lot of that creativity is squeezed out of many of us. We find ourselves either consciously or unconsciously resigning ourselves into one of two groupings: "creatives" or "noncreatives." Because of the importance that having creative employees has on business, there has been a new push in the corporate world to get people to move themselves out of feeling like a noncreative and into being a creative. The new view is that the key isn't teaching people creativity. It is to help them *rediscover* their creative confidence — the natural ability to come up with new ideas and the courage to try them out.

It is this creative confidence that we want to try to instill in our children now, when it is easier to sway them into the "creative" category and not wait for them to experience twenty-or-so more years of social conformity when their thinking has become even more rigid.

Title: **Monster Dude**   Incomplete Figure Task

Alexx

"Many scientists think that philosophy has no place, so, for me, it's a sad time because the role of reflection, contemplation, meditation, self-inquiry, insight, intuition, imagination, creativity, free will, is in a way not given any importance, which is the domain of philosophers."

— Deepak Chopra (Famous, alternative-medicine guru)

Chapter Nine

Creative Development Process in Children

Creativity is a process. The precursors of adult creativity can clearly be seen in young children. Children go through several stages in the Creative Development Process. They are:

EXPLORATION — Baby/Toddler

The creative process starts even as a baby. Once they are able to crawl around and explore objects, they can start to creatively put various objects together — placing objects together, piling them up, making sounds with them, and playing with them. It is important for parents to provide various textures, shapes, and colors in the items their children play with. Alison Gopnik, author of *The Philosophical Baby*, asserts that babies are born experimental scientists who take in scrolls of information by trying things on their own and tweaking as they go. Being more hands-off, as parents, helps kids figure out how to problem-solve and create in their own unique ways.

IDEA GENERATION — Preschool Until Early Elementary

In dealing with young children, the focus should be on the *process* — developing and generating original ideas. Idea generation is the basis of creative potential and, therefore, a critical feature of the creative process. A four-year-old, when listing all the things that are red, will include not only wagons and apples but also chicken pox and cold hands. In order to encourage this process, it is crucial for parents to show acceptance of multiple ideas in a nonevaluative atmosphere. This will help children generate more ideas. A nonevaluation atmosphere is critical in avoiding what Donald Treffinger labels as the "right answer fixation."[14]

Through the socialization process, children move toward conformity during the elementary school years. The percentage of original responses in idea-generation tasks drops from about 50 percent on average for four-year-olds to 25 percent during elementary school. During this stage, parents should encourage and provide opportunities for their children to explore open-ended questions. Parents can directly influence the development of creativity in their children by promoting fantasy in play and curiosity in the early childhood years.[15]

SELF-EVALUATION — Later Elementary to Early High School

Idea generation is still very important, but children in this stage also start to realize that some of their ideas may work better than others. The outcome of the creative process becomes more important to them as well. They start to explore their abilities to generate and evaluate their hypotheses and can now revise their ideas based on that evaluation. It is important for parents to allow their children to evaluate their own ideas and not evaluate their ideas for them.

At this stage, parents should continue encouraging the exploration of open-ended questions, but now also allow their children the space to evaluate the answers they come up with. Promoting "idea generation" is still very important, but add in some fun, problem-solving activities that have more than one creative solution.

EVALUATION BY OTHERS — Later High School to Adulthood

In this stage, adolescents are ready for more complex, creative problem solving. Encourage them to push the boundaries of idea generation. They can also take on more complex problems in general that go beyond personal or educational issues and can extend into societal issues. They can also use a number of creative-thinking strategies in conjunction with each other.

Only in this later adolescent and adulthood stage should there be evaluation of ideas by others for the creative-development process to be as uninhibited and nurtured as much as possible.

Title: **Under the sea**   Incomplete Figure Task

Bailey

"The human brain had a vast memory storage. It made us curious and very creative. Those were the characteristics that gave us an advantage — curiosity, creativity, and memory. And, that brain did something very special. It invented an idea called 'the future.'"

— David Suzuki (a Canadian academic, science broadcaster, and environmental activist)

Chapter Ten

Steps to Creative Thinking

N ow that we've established the importance of helping your children develop their Creative Intelligence; how do you help them do that? First, you need to know how Creative Thinking Works. There are *five* steps to Creative Thinking: 1) Formulate the Question, 2) Gather Information, 3) Generate Ideas, 4) Analyze Solutions, and 5) Take Action. I will break the steps down for you here and then go into some of the steps in more detail in the following chapters.

STEP 1   Formulate the Question

Whether it's a problem your child needs to solve, a homework assignment project they have, an essay they need to write, or something they want to create, the first step is to have them fully examine the problem, issue, or task at hand and frame a question around it.

They should think of all the different viewpoints and perspectives they could take when they are faced with coming up with a "solution" or "end product." They should examine the problem in different ways. For instance, if they are deciding "What would be cool to paint?" they could try looking at it from another angle: "What could I paint that would evoke the emotion of excitement?" Or, if they are answering an essay question like "Who is your hero, and why?" they could think of the question as, "What character trait do you admire most in people, and what person can you think of who exemplifies that trait?" Or, if it is a project they are assigned on Native Americans, have them think of all the different approaches they could take — family, traditions, jobs, environment, point-of-view from a child in the tribe, or from an elder, or from a descendant, etc.

Once they have framed the issue/problem into a multisided question, it is time to move on to the next step of pulling information from their knowledge base, experiences, and research. That is the Gather Information step.

STEP 2   Gather Information

This step is second nature to us. We are curious creatures by nature. In this step, the "issue/problem" they are trying to solve is further explored by getting themselves prepared to brainstorm by collecting as much knowledge as they can on the subject. Research can manifest itself in many different ways. They can do research on the computer, in books, from school material, or they can tap into their experiences with the world — places they've visited, or stories from ancestors. They can collect any information that they can think of that might help them with the next step of generating ideas around the question they formulated.

However, it is important to know when to stop researching and move on to the next step. You can get caught up in this stage — so you have to know when enough is enough, and when it's time to move on.

STEP 3 Generate Ideas

This is where they take all the knowledge they have gathered and use it as a starting point to brainstorm on possible solutions. This is called **Divergent Thinking**. They should think outside the box — no idea is too outlandish. No idea should be discarded or critiqued at this point. This is the step where creativity really comes into play. They need to use their imagination and knowledge. They must not stop with just what the obvious answer might be. Much of creativity is about making new connections between existing ideas.

As your children come up with their list of ideas in this step, you want to encourage the following traits:

FLUENCY — number of ideas generated
ORIGINALITY — how unique the ideas are
FLEXIBILITY — how many different areas the ideas cover
ELABORATION — how detailed the ideas are

Once they have exhausted their idea generation — even having taken a moment to step away from it and come back — it is then time to organize the ideas/solutions they have generated.

STEP 4   Analyze Solutions

In this step, your children will take all of the ideas they have come up with and evaluate them to decide which is the best idea or solution for the problem, issue, or task at hand. This is called **Convergent Thinking**. Once a sufficient amount of ideas has been explored, convergent thinking can be used. Knowledge, logic, probabilities, and other decision-making strategies are taken into consideration as the solutions are evaluated individually in a search for a single, best answer, which, when reached, is unambiguous. Evaluating means analyzing and judging, picking apart ideas, and sorting them into piles of good and bad, useful and useless.

The deductive logic that the fictional character Sherlock Holmes used is a good example of convergent thinking. Gathering various tidbits of facts and data, he was able to put the pieces of a puzzle together and come up with a logical answer to the question: Who done it?

It's important not to jump ahead too soon to this step. Most people evaluate too soon and too often and, therefore, create less. In order to create more and better ideas, your children must separate creation from evaluation, coming up with lots of ideas first and then judging their worth later.

STEP 5   Take Action

Once they have decided on a solution, they must make an action plan in order to carry out the solution. Many great, creative ideas are lost to us because this final step is not taken, and the idea never gets to see the light of day. This is where the final push comes. The solution/idea that they have come up with must now be broken down into action steps in order for it to be implemented. The solution should be sketched out, and an action plan needs to be outlined.

This is where the "creator" must shut out all the naysayers and forge ahead. Once they have put a stake in the ground and decided on a solution/idea, they must not look for all the reasons they shouldn't pursue it if they really feel passionate about their decision. Oftentimes, it is at this stage that an idea gets derailed, due mostly to outside influences that shake a person's confidence or to a lack of discipline to follow through on the idea.

They should beware of sharing their idea and looking for approval from someone they would consider an "expert" on the subject. Expect the "experts" to be negative. The more expert and specialized a person becomes, the narrower their mindset becomes. Experts will spend all their time showing and explaining why it can't be done and why it can't work. This is why when Fred Smith created Federal Express, every delivery expert in the US predicted it would never survive. They believed if this delivery concept was doable, the Post Office or UPS would have done it long ago.

Finally, after they have implemented a solution, encourage your children to evaluate if the solution worked the way in which it was intended to work. If it didn't work, have your children decide if they feel the need to go back and choose another alternative solution. If at first you don't succeed, try, try, try again.

WALT DISNEY'S CREATIVE THINKING STRATEGY

It is said that film producer and innovator Walt Disney used to think up and refine ideas by breaking the process into three distinct chunks: the dreamer, the realist, and the spoiler (or critic).

The Dreamer

This stage was for fantasizing — creating the most fantastic and absurd ideas possible. This stage was about "Why not?"

The Realist

As the Realist, the Dreamer ideas would be reexamined and reworked into something more practical. It wasn't about the reasons it could not be achieved, but only about what would be necessary if it *could* be done. This stage is about "How?"

The Spoiler

In this third stage, he would become the critic... shooting holes in the ideas he had come up with. It is said that the ideas that survived this process were the ones Walt would work on.

By compartmentalizing the stages, Walt didn't let reality get in the way of the dream step. The realist was allowed to work without the harsh filter of a spoiler. And, the spoiler spends time examining a well-thought-out idea... something with a bit more structure.

When we brainstorm alone and in groups — too often — we tend to fill the room with a dreamer or two, a few realists, and a bunch of spoilers. In these conditions, dream ideas don't stand a chance.

There is additional information that Walt went further, moving from one room to another as he shifted thinking, using different spaces specifically for each stage.

Title: **Potato Patato Tomato Tamato**   Incomplete Figure Task

Alexx

"In an era of parental paranoia, lawsuit mania, and testing frenzy, we are failing to inspire our children's curiosity, creativity, and imagination. We are denying them opportunities to tinker, discover, and explore — in short, to play."

— Darrell Hammond (comedian, actor, and former, long-standing cast member of *Saturday Night Live*)

Chapter Eleven
Divergent Thinking

ivergent Thinking, used in the *Generate Ideas* stage, is the most critical step in creative thinking. It is thinking outward instead of inward — the ability to see lots of answers to a question and lots of ways of interpreting a question. Divergent thinking typically occurs in a spontaneous, free-flowing manner, where many creative ideas are generated and evaluated. Multiple possible solutions are explored in a short amount of time, and unexpected connections are drawn.

BRAINSTORMING

Brainstorming is "...a group problem-solving technique that involves the spontaneous contribution of ideas from all members of the group; *also:* the mulling over of ideas by one or more individuals in an attempt to devise or find a solution to a problem..." (*Merriam-Webster Dictionary*).

Advertising executive Alex F. Osborn began developing methods for creative problem-solving in 1939. He was frustrated by employees' inability to develop creative ideas individually for ad campaigns. In response, he began hosting group-thinking sessions and discovered a significant improvement in the quality and quantity of ideas produced by employees. Osborn popularized the term "brainstorming" in his 1963 book *Applied Imagination*. He created four main rules of Brainstorming:

1. **Focus on quantity:** This rule is based on the idea that *quantity breeds quality*. The assumption is that the greater the number of ideas generated, the greater the chance of producing a radical and effective solution.

2. **Withhold criticism:** In brainstorming, criticism of ideas generated should be put "on hold." Instead, participants should focus on extending or adding to ideas, reserving criticism for a later "critical stage" of the process. By suspending judgment, participants will feel free to generate unusual ideas.

3. **Welcome unusual ideas:** To get a good and long list of ideas, unusual ideas are welcomed. Ideas can be generated by looking at the problem from new perspectives and suspending assumptions. These new ways of thinking may provide better solutions.

4. **Combine and improve ideas:** Good ideas may be combined to form a single, better good idea.

IMAGINATION

To be a good brainstormer, you need to have a good imagination. Albert Einstein said, "The true sign of intelligence is not knowledge, but imagination." Facts and figures can take you only so far if you can't "think outside the box" and imagine different ways in which to use that information. Think about it. Where would we be without innovation? And, innovation comes from our imagination, our ability to picture things that don't currently exist in reality. All great creative thinkers are using their imagination. What they are doing in addition to that is making links between things so they are associating. So, the two big, key words when it comes to creativity are "imagination" and "association." What you have to do when you are being creative is find those associations and connections between things that are going to create something new.

Children who actively use their imagination reap a host of benefits, according to Dorothy Singer, professor of psychology at Yale University. In her book *The House of Make Believe: Children's Play and the Developing Imagination* she outlines these benefits:

* Imagination helps school-age children solve problems by helping them think through different outcomes to various situations and role-playing ways to cope with difficult or new circumstances.
* Imagination allows children to practice real-life skills. From shopping at a pretend grocery store to assigning roles and dialogue to dolls or puppets, children's pretend play helps

them practice and apply new learning and better understand how those skills are used in the real world.

- Imagination encourages a rich vocabulary. Telling and hearing real or made-up stories, reading books and pretend play help children learn and retain new words.
- Imagination helps children grow up to be adults who are creative thinkers. Adults who were imaginative children often become problem solvers, innovators, and creative thinkers.

OUTSIDE THE BOX THINKING

When talking about creative problem-solving, many times the term "think outside the box" will be mentioned. In order for our children to learn how to "think outside the box," they first need to realize that things "outside the box" do exist. The first step is to teach them how to notice things in a concrete object that are beyond what they readily see when they first look at it. They need to expand the scope of their vision. They need to practice the art of looking for things that aren't glaringly obvious. This will help them to realize that they shouldn't just be looking "inside the box"; they should also be looking "outside the box," "on the box," "around the box," "behind the box," and "next to the box." Once they get in the habit of really studying an object from all angles in order to learn as much about it as possible, they can then take that same approach at looking at less concrete things — such as "problems." This will then lead to their ability, when faced with a problem, not to stop at the first solution that comes to them when trying to solve it, but instead to believe that there could be other possibilities beyond the obvious, and to motivate them to keep looking or thinking for other possible, better solutions. This will result in them becoming more creative problem-solvers.

Have your children pick out a random object around the house. First, at arm's length from it and without touching it, have them list all the details they notice about the object. The next step is to have them pick the object up and turn it over in their hands and really study it. Encourage them to look at it closely, from all angles. Now, have them list any additional details they hadn't noticed about the object before they really explored it. "Extra points" for them if they tell you a detail about the object that even *you* didn't know about. It might be a button on a remote control that they hadn't seen before, a warning label on a bottle, or a nonslip surface on the bottom of a jar. Explain to them how, by really looking at something from all sides, they can learn something new about it that they didn't notice at first glance. Have them do this a few times with different objects to get them used to the art of "seeing beyond the obvious."

Later on, when you see them having trouble solving a problem, whether it's a homework problem or a personal one, refer back to this activity, and place an object in their hand. Ask them to remember exploring this object, and have them once again turn it over and around in their hands and study it carefully. Now, tell them to do the same thing in their mind with the problem they are trying to solve. If it's a homework problem, have them go back and look more closely at the question or the reading passage and see if they can pick something new up that they hadn't noticed the first time they looked at it. If it's a personal problem, ask them to look at the problem from different "angles," different "points of view" — see if, by having them work at looking outside and around the problem ("outside the box"), this helps clear the block they are having to solving it and open up new solutions for them.

FLUENCY

Fluency is all about generating a lot of different ideas. It is a valuable skill to practice because, when children have many different ideas, you have more options and are, therefore, more likely to find more, viable solutions to your problem. In addition, often one idea leads to another; so, by generating many ideas, children are allowing that process to flow naturally. Question start-ups to promote fluency include: "In what ways...," "List...," or "Brainstorm...." Examples are: "In what ways might we solve the lunch-line problem?" "List different forms of transportation." "Brainstorm possible consequences of global warming."

How fast children can generate a quantity of ideas is a skill they can develop just by playing at it. Faster speed at that kind of productivity is one of the hallmarks of creative genius.

ORIGINALITY

Originality of thought is the ability to generate new, different, and unique ideas that others are not likely to generate. If someone asks your children what can they use a coat hanger for, and they answer "for hanging a coat," that would not get them high points in creativity. If they said they could use it to take better pictures of outdoor flowers by using a wire-hanger loop wrapped in a shower curtain to diffuse the sunlight, well, that is *much* more unique. Original responses usually occur at the end of an idea-finding activity, after the more obvious ideas have been produced. Question start-ups for originality include: "What is the most unusual idea... or the most unusual way...?" and "What if...?" For example: "What is the most unusual way to use a straw?" and "What if we had no electricity?"

FLEXIBILITY

Flexibility is the ability to create different categories of ideas and to perceive an idea from different points of view. Most people tend to focus on one way — "This is the way I think; this is the way I see that" — when it should be "How many ways can I see this? How many perspectives can I look at it from?" The great creative thinkers play with looking at things from different perspectives. Flexibility requires generating a wide range of ideas. The flexibility question start-up ""How many different ways...?" encourages a child's flexibility. "How many different ways can you find to clean up your room?" or "List many different structures you can create with blocks," are questions that encourage flexibility in children's responses.

ELABORATION

Elaboration is the ability to expand on an idea by embellishing it with details or to improve or rework the idea. Elaboration allows a person to "fill in" or add to information. It requires adding ideas, providing details, extending thinking. "What else...?" is a question start-up leading to inquiries like "What else do you see?" followed by a probe, "Tell me more."

A more specific way to give detail is to include words that relate to the five senses: sight, touch, taste, sound, and smell.

Similes and metaphors are also elaboration strategies that compare one thing to another thing. Remember, similes are comparisons that use "like" or "as" to describe two things. "He runs as fast as a cheetah." Metaphors are comparisons that say one thing *is* another thing. "My emotions were an icy river of cold feelings."

Title: **Duck Pond**   Incomplete Figure Task

Alexx

"You can't just give someone a creativity injection. You have to create an environment for curiosity and a way to encourage people and get the best out of them."

— Sir Ken Robinson (English author, speaker, and international advisor on education in the arts to the government)

Chapter Twelve

Divergent Thinking Techniques

There are a number of Divergent Thinking Techniques. Some of the main techniques are: Mind Mapping, Free Association, Attribute Analysis, and Empathy Design.

MIND MAPPING

A **mind map** is a diagram used to visually outline a person's brainstorming session. Your children can create a mind map around the problem they are trying to solve or the issue they are addressing by writing that problem/issue in a circle in the center of a piece of paper. They can now draw lines off of that circle and label those lines with associated ideas, words, and concepts. Major categories come off of the central circle, and lesser categories are sub-branches of larger branches. Categories can represent words, ideas, tasks, research ideas, or other items related to a central, key word or idea. Mind maps foster creativity by helping your children see both existing connections and connections that might be missing.

The following list is a guideline for creating mind maps suggested by Tony Buzan, who popularized the term:

1. Have your children start in the center with an image/ words of the topic, using at least three colors.

2. Have them use images, symbols, and codes throughout their mind map.

3. Have them select key words, and print using upper or lower case letters.

4. Each word/image is best alone and sitting on its own line.

5. The lines should be connected, starting from the central image. The central lines are thicker and organic, and, then, they should get thinner as they radiate out from the center.

6. Have them make the lines the same length as the word/ image they support.

7. Have them use multiple colors throughout the mind map, for visual stimulation and also to encode or group.

8. Have them develop their own personal style of mind mapping.

9. Have them use emphasis and show associations in their mind map.

10. Keep the mind map clear by using radial hierarchy, numerical order, or outlines to embrace branches.

FREE ASSOCIATION

Free association is similar to brainstorming, yet there is one major difference. In brainstorming, your children are listing and compiling ideas. *With free association, they focus on individual words or symbols.*

If you say the word "apple," what is the first word that pops into their mind? And, what word do they think of when they write down that word? And, so on. The process of free association is a way to get your children to go beyond a topic and explore how things are associated (*or related*) in their mind.

The same method also works for pictures or symbols. Have them draw a simple picture, or give them a sample drawing to start with. Then, have them draw whatever picture they think of when they look at that first drawing. Next, have them draw a picture that is related to the second one they drew, etc.

ATTRIBUTE ANALYSIS

This is a technique used to investigate and improve tangible things. Have your children take an item, *such as a camera*, and list all the attributes of that item that they can think of. List parts, functions, features, bonuses, and every characteristic of the item.

Then they can start asking questions that could lead to ways in which the item could be improved, combined with another thing, simplified, added to, or phased out of use.

Think of all the ways the simple camera has been changed over the years. Without creative thinking, no one would have put a camera inside a phone, made it digital, created ones that could go underwater, or simplified them so even a child could use them.

EMPATHIC DESIGN

Design empathy is an approach that draws upon people's real-world experiences to address modern challenges. When a person allows a deep, emotional understanding of people's needs to inspire them and transform their work, they unlock the creative capacity for innovation.

The definition of "empathy" is the ability to be aware of, understanding of, and sensitive to another person's feelings and thoughts without necessarily having had the same experience. Empathic design was presented as a process that involved observation, data collection and analysis, and prototyping. Most significantly, the discipline was identified as a way to uncover people's unspoken, latent needs and then address them through design (Leonard and Rayport, 1997) — by responding to real, but unexpressed and unmet needs.

Empathy is a powerful force. Research shows that when we are empathetic, we enhance our ability to receive and process information. Putting ourselves in someone else's shoes — a part of our subconscious behavior — causes measurable changes in our cognitive style, increasing our so-called field-dependent thinking. This type of thinking helps us put information in context and pick up contextual cues from the environment, which is essential when we're seeking to understand how things relate to one another, literally and figuratively. Research also shows that we are more helpful and generous after an empathic encounter (Decety and Ickes, 2011).

Once empathy is achieved, it needs to be moderated: apply too much and our creative thinking loses focus; apply too little and the depth of our creative insight suffers.

It's possible to fuel empathy experiences, without a lot of effort. For example, if a product marketer had to come up with a long-term vision for a brand of toys, they could look to market research and just study a bunch of numbers. Or, they could utilize empathic design and do something as simple as getting on the floor for a play-along with youngsters in the target age range and be able to really connect to the mindset of children.

In this technique, people go out into the world and immerse themselves in the issue they are trying to solve. They gather information by observing users, manufacturers, anyone who has a touch point with the issue. When IDEO, an innovative design firm in California that uses Empathic Design, was tasked with inventing a new shopping cart, they went out to find out what the people who use, make, and repair shopping carts really think. They went to a grocery store and watched how shoppers used the cart, observed safety issues while watching children climb on and in the cart, watched shoppers check out and even unload their groceries at their car. Finding these real-life experts would enable your children to learn much more quickly than if they tried to learn all this information on their own.

SCAMPER

Scamper is a strategy that can be used to break mind-set and enhance creative thinking (Eberle, 1987). SCAMPER is set up as a mnemonic acronym that provides a structured way to stimulate divergent thinking, imagination, originality, and intuition. First proposed by Alex Osborne in 1953, this thinking strategy was further developed by Bob Eberle and noted in his 1971 book *SCAMPER: Games for Imagination Development*. Eberle states that, much as the word "scamper" suggests "running playfully about as a child," the strategy SCAMPER may also evoke the need "to run playfully about in one's mind in search of ideas" (Eberle, 1984).

Each of the letters in the acronym SCAMPER stands for a stage in the process of trying to look at and dissect a problem/issue in different ways in order to spur on more creative ideas. Have your children think about their topic of concern and ask, "To create a unique solution, what might we...

Substitute? — person? place? thing? (Substitution is a trial-and-error method whereby you can try things out, see if they work, then try something different.)

Combine? — what? combine purposes? ideas? (Combining involves synthesis, the process of combining previous ideas or things together to create something new.)

Adapt? — reshape? tune up? tone down? (Think about what is already known about the problem and how others are solving it. Become aware of the processes others are using.)

Modify? — magnify? minimize? (When you modify and alter something, you reflect on what is needed to support and make it better, greater, simpler, or even more complex. Magnifying will concentrate on making things bigger, thicker, stronger, or more intense. Minimizing will concentrate on making things lighter, slower, less frequent, or reduced in some capacity.)

Put to other uses? — new use? (Consider ways that the target can be used other than originally intended.)

Eliminate or Elaborate? — remove? omit? simplify? embellish? (To remove or omit part or all of a particular quality. If using elaborate, to add more details.)

Rearrange? — change order? plan? scheme? (Consider how the change of order or sequence would affect the target or challenge.)

Thomas Edison believed that every new idea is some addition or modification to something that already exists. You take a subject and manipulate or change it into something else. Edison studied all his inventions and ideas as springboards for other inventions and ideas. To Edison, the telephone (sounds transmitted) suggested the phonograph (sounds recorded), which suggested motion pictures (images recorded). Once asked to describe the key to creativity, he reportedly said to never quit working on your subject until you get what you're after.

Title: __Butterfly Garden__   Incomplete Figure Task

Alexx

"I'm very anti-schedule. Except for board meetings, I don't really schedule things or keep a calendar. I think appointments are caustic to creativity."

> — David Karp (American web developer, entrepreneur, and founder of the short-form, blogging platform *Tumblr*)

Chapter Thirteen

When Your Children Get Stuck

When one brainstorms, it's normal to first come up with obvious answers that are less unique. These may not always be the best solutions. So, it's important to encourage your children not to stop at the first moment they get stuck when trying to come up with a new idea, and to, instead, push ahead. Here are a few ideas that can help keep your children going when they think they have exhausted their list of ideas. It is at this point where their creative genius can really come out if they just keep forging ahead. Encourage them to:

- Persevere! Keep trying different strategies, and stay open to creative ideas. Try not to get frustrated.
- Be more active in the solution! Ask themselves questions about the problem. Draw sketches of what they think the solution should look like.
- Do more research! Remember: Much of creativity is just a new way of connecting existing ideas. Researching their topic on the Internet might provide them with ideas that may inspire them to make new connections.
- Break the problem into parts. Analyze the parts of the problem. Have your children concentrate on the parts of the problem they understand and can solve.
- Paraphrase. Redescribe the problem. Think of simpler ways to describe the problem. Have them ask other classmates or family members to describe the problem to them in their own words.
- Take a break. Incubate. Your children's subconscious will work on the problem while they do something else, like exercising, talking to friends, or just relaxing. Sometimes all they need is a break to achieve that final breakthrough.
- Try using a different strategy. There is usually more than one way to solve a problem, and they may find a method that they haven't considered may generate more ideas than the one they're using currently.
- Talk to others. Sometimes, if they verbalize the problem to someone else, that person can steer them in a direction that they hadn't thought of and thus stimulate a whole new set of ideas for them.
- Get outside. Take a break from solitude. Sometimes being in a different environment will spark new ideas.

- Set a time limit. If they set a timer for their brainstorming session, this will help remove the feeling of being overwhelmed by the process.
- Look at the problem in a different way. Taking a different point of view can provide them with new insight that maybe they hadn't seen before.
- Create a psychological distance. Have them pretend they are trying to solve someone else's problem. This will help them to avoid simply solving the problem in their usual way. If it's a paper your children are writing, have them think of it as a paper they are writing for someone else.
- Separate work from creativity. Don't research and try to be creative at the same time. Encourage them to do their brainstorming away from the computer.
- Use counterfactual thinking. Think about what could be added or taken away from the situation.

Title: The farm   Incomplete Figure Task

Brady

"The best ideas come as jokes. Make your thinking as funny as possible."

— David Ogilvy (founder of Ogilvy & Mather, a Manhattan-based international advertising, marketing, and public relations agency)

Chapter Fourteen

Convergent Thinking

Once your children's brainstorming session is over, they must now decide which solution is the best one out of all the ones that were generated. It is at this *Analyze Solutions* step that judgment and critique come into play. This would be Walt Disney's "Spoiler" stage — where your children become the critic and weigh and measure each possible solution they have come up with in a structured way, so that they can come to a conclusion about which solution is the most realistic, the most useful, and can be implemented in a practical way.

One way you can help children evaluate their possible solutions is by teaching them a technique called the "Six Thinking Hats" method, invented by Dr. Edward de Bono in the early 1980s.

We all know what it means to "put our thinking hat on," but thinking about something creatively involves wearing more than just one hat. The "Six Thinking Hats" method involves looking at a problem from six differing perspectives. By doing this, you can produce more ideas than if you had looked at the situation from only one or two points of view.

To help children really understand the thought process, the first time (or couple of times) through I like to take the Six Hats method literally. Collect six hats from around the house, each with a different predominate color from the following list: red, white, yellow, black, green, and blue. The type of hat is not important — they can be all different types. With every hat you place on their heads, tell the children in what way that colored hat is going to help them evaluate the possible solutions they have come up with, in order to get to the best one.

Red Hat: Look at the situation emotionally — share feelings and fears. What do your feelings tell you?

White Hat: Look at the situation objectively — gather your information. What are all the facts?

Yellow Hat: Probe for the value and benefits of solutions under consideration. Which parts of the solutions will work?

Black Hat: Devil's advocate perspective. Which parts of the solutions are you considering won't work?

Green Hat: Think creatively. What are some new possibilities and better alternative ideas?

Blue Hat: Think broadly, pulling from all of your hats. What is the best overall solution?

The more you can encourage your children to use this multifaceted approach to creatively solve a problem, the better they will become at it. Eventually, they will realize that they can "wear more than one hat" at the same time. It will be a skill that will serve them well all of their lives.

After listing at least three potential solutions, your children should identify at least one "pro" and one "con" for each option. They can use a graphic organizer like the one below:

Problem _____

Possible Solutions	Pros	Cons

My Solution _____

Teach your children (through modeling using the graphic organizer) how to choose solutions that will most likely solve a problem with:

- the time and resources available
- minimal (or no) negative impact on themselves or others (now or in the future)

Once a solution has been chosen, it's time to act. Will the solution be implemented immediately? If not, when and how?

Title: **House Of Happiness**   Incomplete Figure Task

Bailey

"Everything in life is writable about if you have the outgoing guts to do it, and the imagination to improvise. The worst enemy to creativity is self-doubt."

— Sylvia Plath (American poet, novelist, and short-story writer)

Chapter Fifteen

Other Ideas for Improving Your Children's Creativity

LET THEM GET BORED

According to Dr. Laura Markham,[16] parents often respond to kids' boredom by providing structured activities or technological entertainment. But, unstructured time challenges kids to engage with themselves and the world, to imagine and invent and create. Kids need practice with unstructured time, or they will never learn to manage it.

Even more importantly, children need empty time to explore, which is the beginning of creativity. So, how should you respond when your kids complain that they're bored? Help them brainstorm about possible activities, but make it clear that it's their job to figure out how to enjoy their own time.

TIME TO THINK

When your children are trying to come up with an idea for a school project, instead of spending all their time on the Internet researching for ideas, have them take a moment to unplug. Let them spend some quiet time by themselves to come up with some ideas. Dorothea Brande, in her classic *Becoming A Writer* writes, "Prisoners who never wrote a word in the days of their freedom will write on any paper they can lay hands on." Having time by oneself being lost in thought is one of the pillars of creativity.

HAVE THEM EXERCISE

We all know that kids benefit from regular exercise in many physical and emotional ways, but now research shows that regular exercise can also boost creativity. A new study in the journal *Frontiers in Human Neuroscience* shows that regular exercisers do better on tests of creativity than their more sedentary peers. To determine the association between exercise and creativity, researchers had forty-eight athletes (who exercised at least four times a week) and forty-eight nonathletes (who didn't regularly exercise) do a creativity test. Researchers found that the regular exercisers did better on the creativity test than those who didn't regularly exercise.

The three elements of fitness are endurance (aerobic activity), strength, and flexibility. Just to be healthy, every child should get at least sixty minutes of physical activity a day — add a bit more over the course of the week for an additional creativity boost. "Exercising on a regular basis may act as a cognitive enhancer, promoting creativity in inexpensive and healthy ways," stated study researcher Lorenza Colzato, a cognitive psychologist at Leiden University in the Netherlands.

A *Psychology Today* article explains the connection between exercise and creativity like this: "Sweat is like WD-40 for your mind — it lubricates the rusty hinges of your brain and makes your thinking more fluid. Exercise allows your conscious mind to access fresh ideas that are buried in the subconscious".[17]

So, get your kids up off the couch and get them moving. RUN. JUMP. CREATE.

LET THEM BE MESSY

Since tidiness has been associated with upholding societal standards, Kathleen D. Vohs, a professor of marketing at the Carlson School of Management at the University of Minnesota, predicted that just being around tidiness would elicit a desire for convention.[18] She and her colleagues also predicted the opposite: that being around messiness would lead people away from convention, in favor of new directions.

Forty-eight research subjects came individually to their laboratory and were assigned to messy or tidy rooms. They told subjects to imagine that a ping-pong ball factory needed to think of new uses for ping-pong balls and to write down as many ideas as they could. Answers were judged for degree of creativity. Those answers deemed low in creativity included using ping-pong balls for beer-pong, a well-known party game. Answers rated high in creativity included using ping-pong balls as ice cube trays, and attaching them to chair legs to protect floors.

The subjects in both types of rooms came up with about the same number of ideas, however, the messy-room subjects were more creative, as was expected. Not only were their ideas 28 percent more creative on average, but they also came up with almost five times the number of ideas that were judged as "highly creative" than did their tidy-room counterparts.

So, next time your children say they don't want to clean their rooms, maybe it's not such a bad thing.

LET THEM NAP

A poll of some of businesses' most creative people conducted by the magazine *Fast Company* highlighted that a common piece of advice to bring out creativity was variations on "take more naps."

Thomas Edison was known to take naps. He would sleep sitting upright in his chair, elbow propped on the arm with a handful of marbles. He would think about his problem until he fell asleep, and, upon doing so, he would drop the marbles on the floor. When the noise woke him up, Edison wrote down whatever was in his head, regardless of what it was — creative solutions, new ideas, a reminder to pick up milk on the way home.

We often end up with strong, visual images lingering from our dreams when we wake out of REM sleep, when most of our dreaming happens. For this reason, lots of artists try to take advantage of this just-waking-up period to improve their creative thinking.

Famous surrealist painter Salvador Dalí was also known for using this state to help him generate creative ideas. He would often nap in a chair, holding a spoon in his hand. When he drifted off to sleep, he'd drop the spoon, and the noise it made would wake him up, helping him to capture the vivid images of his dreams.

HAVE THEM TAKE A WALK

According to a study by researchers, Marily Oppezzo and Daniel Schwartz, at Stanford University (Stanford Report, 2014), there may be a reason people walk back and forth, or pace, when they are trying to think of a new idea. In a study of nearly 180 participants, it was found that a person's creative output increased by an average of 60 percent when walking.

The researchers also discovered that those who walked more consistently were able to write down more creative answers on tests than did the individuals who were sitting before the time that they took the tests.

A *Fast Company* poll found that even the most creative people get stuck and need a way to refocus or unfocus to get back on track. Many of the people polled stated that they were inspired by physical movement — either actual exercise — like going for a walk — or even dancing or taking a hike.

TRAVEL

To cultivate creativity, you want to increase your children's chances of stumbling upon an unexpected link. You are more likely to find an unusual solution when you have been exposed to more experiences. So, the more you can introduce different cultural and environmental stimuli (whether by crossing international or just state borders), the more information your children are accumulating.

One study[19] showed that, for college students, those who traveled abroad scored higher on creative-thinking tests than those who stayed at their main campus. This particular study followed students who traveled from their college in the US to take part in a summer study program in England. The researcher concluded that foreign travel exposed these students to novel experiences that enhanced their creativity.

DIM THE LIGHTS

New German research finds a darkened room encourages freedom of thought and inspires innovation. "Darkness increases freedom from constraints, which in turn promotes creativity," report Anna Steidle of the University of Stuttgart and Lioba Werth of the University of Hohenheim. A dimly lit environment, they explain in the *Journal of Environmental Psychology*, "elicits a feeling of freedom, self-determination, and reduced inhibition," all of which encourage innovative thinking. During that all-important phase when you're grasping for ideas, dim light appears to be a catalyst for creativity. "Darkness changes a room's visual message," the researchers explain, and one such message seems to be it's safe to explore widely and let your imagination run free.

The researchers did note, however, that innovation consists of two distinct phases: generating ideas, and then analyzing and implementing them. The latter requires analytical thinking, and, in a final experiment, where Convergent Thinking was involved, participants did better on that task when they were in a brightly lit room rather than a dimly lit one. "Creativity may begin in the dark," Steidle and Werth write, "but it shouldn't end there."

DESIGN A CREATIVE ENVIRONMENT

Every space is a stage in which we play out our life, and it tells us what role we play and how we should act. Classrooms full of stationary rows of desks and offices full of aisles of cubicles give out the message that you need to keep to yourself and be quiet. Instead, you want to provide your children with an environment that gives the message that innovation, creativity, and playfulness are valued there.

Research shows that large, open rooms with high ceilings can also promote creative thinking. You should set up playrooms and study rooms more like a kindergarten, with lots of manipulatives and lots of things to prototype — this is how the Creative Class at Stanford University has set up their classroom.

Decorate with innovative, imaginative items. When children are trying to come up with creative ideas, they tend to look around the room they are in for inspiration. Physical environments designed to stimulate the senses can enhance creative problem solving. For example, when shown an object in the shape of a semi-circle and asked, "What can we use this for?" children will exhaust their first mental images and begin developing ideas from what they see in their surroundings. Looking around a classroom or playroom for cues is a creative, problem-solving method. An environment that provides both novelty and variety will greatly aid creativity.

These days, kids spend most of their time indoors. So, now it's more important than ever to put thought into designing rooms that will inspire their creativity. There have been many studies that claim different colors enhance different moods. For instance, one study (Dr. Juliet Zhu and Ravi Mehta, University of British Columbia, 2009), found that blue environmental cues prompted twice as many creative outputs as when under a red-color condition. They concluded that, through the association of the color blue with the sky and water, it made people feel open and peaceful, and, therefore, safer about being more creative and exploratory.

Even switching the color of your child's computer background screen can make a difference. Research shows that blue enhances performance on creative tasks, for example, while making it red helps with detail-oriented tasks. So, in the desire to raise more creative kids, maybe you need to rethink painting their rooms that ever-popular eggshell white.

PLAY AMBIENT NOISE

In a series of experiments that looked at the effects of noise on creative thinking, researchers at the University of Illinois at Champaign-Urbana had participants brainstorm ideas for new products while they were exposed to varying levels of background noise. Their results, published in *The Journal of Consumer Research*, found that a level of ambient noise typical of a bustling coffee shop or a television playing in a living room — about seventy decibels — enhanced performance. The reason for this is because quiet tends to sharpen your focus, which can prevent you from thinking in the abstract. But, moderate levels can distract people just enough so that they think more broadly, which can help you think outside the box.

The site called "Coffitivity" was inspired by this research showing that the *"whoosh"* of espresso machines and caffeinated chatter typical of most coffee shops create just the right level of background noise to stimulate creativity. The website, which is free, plays an ambient, coffee-shop soundtrack that, according to researchers, helps people think more creatively.

HAVE THEM SIT OUTSIDE A BOX — LITERALLY

There is new evidence for the power of metaphors in jump-starting creativity, including a study published in *Psychological Science* in 2012. Test participants enacted various metaphors for creativity and then took an association test designed to measure original thinking. (For "thinking outside the box," they actually sat outside a box made from PVC pipe and cardboard.) The results showed that embodying metaphorical creativity did, in fact, enhance it.

New research published in the *Journal of Consumer Psychology* suggests that visual metaphors don't have to be so intrusive to be effective. In one experiment, test participants completed a creativity measure online. During the task, some saw a page banner depicting a brain hovering above a box, while others saw a neutral image (a fish) or none at all. The first group of participants indeed showed better insights than the others; they thought, as it were, outside the box.

BE A ROLE MODEL

Think about your own approach to problem solving. Whether you're aware of it or not, children are always watching you. They observe how you deal with problems as examples of ways they might solve problems themselves. Talk about problem solving. When problems arise in the room, discuss your thought processes as you work through the problem. For example, you might say, "I have a problem. I planned to make pizza tonight, but we don't have any pizza dough. What do you think we should do? Should we use an English Muffin as the base instead? I wonder how that would taste? Should we wait until tomorrow to have pizza because I could buy more dough in the morning? Or, maybe I could ask our neighbor if she has some we could borrow." In other words, model fluid-thinking and a positive attitude as well as a process for solving the small problems of everyday life. And, involve children further by asking them to suggest their own solutions.

Emphasize the vocabulary of problem solving. As you speak with children, use the words "problem," "think," "ideas," and "solve." Children will begin to use them to define and describe their own thinking.

Be willing to make mistakes. It is reassuring to children to discover that adults make mistakes, too. So, let children see some of the mistakes you make, and then ask them to help you solve the resulting problems. They'll feel important and, at the same time, learn that making mistakes isn't really such a bad thing after all. Instead, it's an opportunity for learning (*Scholastic*).

MAKE TIME FOR IMPROVING CREATIVITY

You won't be able to help your children improve their creative talents if you don't make time for them. Schedule some time each week to concentrate on some type of creative project or creativity exercise. Even if it's just for five minutes a day or a longer block of time once a week, making time for enhancing creativity is well worth the reward your children will reap. We often push aside tasks or projects that we know will eat away a chunk of time. But, scheduling a short amount of time and sticking to that time frame isn't so daunting.

The second section of this book is where I provide you with my Creative Mindflexors® — easy creativity-enhancing exercises to use with your children. I have grouped these exercises by the creative skill you will be working on. If you take time out to provide your children with an exercise or two each week — more if you have the time — you will be nurturing their innate creative ability. As Louis Pasteur, the famous French chemist renowned for his discoveries of the principle of vaccinations and the process of milk pasteurization, once said, "Chance favors only the prepared mind." To raise innovative thinkers, you want to foster creativity in their daily lives so that their minds are ready when opportunities arise.

Title: _The Hourglass that the maid dropped_   Incomplete Figure Task

Alexx

"Around here, however, we don't look backwards for very long. We keep moving forward, opening up new doors and doing new things, because we're curious...and curiosity keeps leading us down new paths."

— Walt Disney (an American business magnate,
animator, cartoonist, and director)

Chapter Sixteen

Creative Mindflexors® to Use with Your Children

You must provide lots of hands-on opportunities to engage your children in creative-thinking situations that are age appropriate. Your children's individual learning should be nurtured through individualized learning tasks. As a teaching technique, creative problem solving involves helping children learn how to find answers to puzzles, questions, dilemmas, issues, and social predicaments they face in their daily world.

Children need to learn, repeatedly and on a regular basis, how to think creatively, in order for them to acquire this thinking process. For children younger than five, one-on-one interactions with you, self-exploration, and being provided with items that vary in texture, color, movement, sound, and weight are all they will need to enhance their own inherent, creative foundation.

For your children that are kindergarten through high school age, you can use the Creative Mindflexors® I provide you with in this next section to help them develop all the facets of creative thinking that we have reviewed in this book. You may need to modify some of these activities for the developmental level/age of each child.

I have labeled each Creative Mindflexor with the creative-thinking skill it is meant to enhance. Let's first review those creative skills:

Divergent Thinking (Happens during Brainstorming): The ability to see lots of answers to a question and lots of ways of interpreting questions.

Flexibility: The ability to create different categories of ideas and to perceive an idea from different points of view.

Originality (Imagination and Outside the Box Thinking): The ability to generate new, different, and unique ideas that others are not likely to generate.

Elaboration: The ability to expand on an idea by embellishing it with details or to improve or revise the idea.

Fluency: The ability to generate a lot of different ideas.

Convergent Thinking: The ability to evaluate solutions in search of the single, best answer.

Divergent Thinking
UNUSUAL USES CHALLENGE

Used in the *Torrance Tests of Creative Thinking,* the Unusual Uses Challenge stretches your children's creativity by having them think of as many uses as possible for an everyday object like a chair, coffee mug, tin can, or brick. Here's a sample brainstorm for "paper clip" uses:

- Holds papers together
- Cufflinks
- Earrings
- Bag closure
- Christmas tree ornament hooks
- Bookmark

The test measures *divergent thinking* across four sub-categories:

1. **Fluency** — how many uses you can come up with
2. **Originality** — how uncommon those uses are (e.g., "ornament hook" is more uncommon than "holding papers together")
3. **Flexibility** — how many areas your answers cover (e.g., cufflinks and earrings are both accessories, a.k.a. "one area")
4. **Elaboration** — the amount of detail in your responses

I gave my nine-year-old daughter an empty tissue box and had her write a list of all the uses she could think of for that tissue box. Here is a list of what she came up with:

- Piggy Bank
- Dollhouse
- Shoe
- Hat
- Drum
- Toy guitar
- Train
- Garage for toy cars
- Hair-ribbon holder
- Jewelry box
- Pencil case

This activity will stimulate your children's creativity. Find any object around the house, and give it a try.

A recent book, *1001 Inventions That Changed the World,* by Jack Challoner, looked at innovations both ancient and modern, and found that almost all of them involved either using existing items in a different way or finding new uses for existing items.

Divergent Thinking
IMAGINATION DRAWING STATION

The next four Creative Mindflexors are part of what I call my "Imagination Drawing Station," which is based on one of the most iconic elements of the *Torrance Tests of Creative Thinking* — the Incomplete Figure Task. For children to be able to utilize the fullest extent of their creative ability, it helps for them to know what constitutes creativity, so they can more fully explore it. Creativity is not how well the picture is drawn; it is what they intended for the drawing to represent.

I have listed the criteria researchers use to measure one's creativity in these tasks. Read through the list, and as your children work on the next four activities, give them examples of how they could give more detail to their drawings, in order to show emotion, movement, or humor. Expand your children's creative-thought process to include thinking of the drawing perhaps from a different perspective, or more abstractly. Help them dig deeper into their imagination to go beyond the most logical way to complete the figure (for example: something other than a shark when they see an open triangle), or a more expressive title for their picture. Above all, remember that to nurture is to be supportive. Compliment all of your children's efforts, and use this list to suggest and cultivate, not demand.

1. **Emotional Expressiveness:** Communicating feelings and emotions through titles and drawings. Facial expressions, gestures with hands, a tear, kissing, outstretched arms, etc.
2. **Storytelling Articulateness:** Putting things in context; creating an environment for the object so a story is told.

3. **Movement or Action:** Showing action (rest, stand, sit, lie, run, fly, float, eat, etc.) by implying or stating action through the title or through the figure drawing (position of body, motion of lines).

4. **Expressiveness of Titles:** Transforming visual information into emotions and feelings expressed in words (beyond simple description of drawing).

5. **Synthesis of Incomplete Figures or Lines:** Combining two or more incomplete figures or lines into a bigger drawing.

6. **Unusual Visual Perspective:** Presenting ideas or objects in another view other than the one we would ordinarily see (above, below, at an unusual angle, at different distances, in an unusual position, etc.)

7. **Internal Visualization:** Visualizing beyond the exterior of the object that is being drawn; showing something inside or a cross-section.

8. **Extends or Breaks Borders:** Extending the given lines up, down, or out.

9. **Humor:** Incorporating unusual combinations and surprises. Incorporating fundamental absurdity in human behavior or character; exaggeration; satire; opposites; puns; etc.

10. **Richness of Imagery:** Creating a memorable image through variety, vividness, liveliness, intensity.

11. **Colorfulness of Imagery:** Exciting in its appeal to the senses of taste, touch, smell, sight (flavor, earthiness, unreal, spooky, emotionally appealing, fantastic, etc.).

12. **Fantasy:** Creating a drawing from literature, TV, movies, or original fantasy.

Divergent Thinking
IMAGINATION DRAWING STATION

1. THE INCOMPLETE FIGURE TEST

One of the most iconic elements of the ***Torrance Test of Creative Thinking*** is the *Incomplete Figure Test*. The person is given a drawing that is incomplete, composed of a partial shape, form, or line and is asked to complete the picture using their imagination in the most creative way possible. I call it "imaginating." The more creative child will go beyond the most logical way to complete the figure. They also should give their completed picture an imaginative title. Examples of different types of shapes that can be used are: a partial triangle, a squiggle line, or a semi-circle. It is this Creative Mindflexor that you will find examples of drawn by my children in between each chapter of this book.

For this Creative Mindflexor, take a blank piece of white paper, and draw an unfinished shape for your children. Tell them to use the shape to draw an unusual, interesting picture, and see what they come up with. I started off with the simple, partial triangle. My seven-year-old boy drew a bird, and my nine-year-old daughter turned hers into a cartoon snail.

It's a fun, creative activity to do with your kids. Uncommon subject matter, implied stories, humor, and original perspective all show high levels of creativity. Try to encourage your children to communicate a feeling, show movement, and include rich imagery in their drawings.

This Creative Mindflexor is not only fun to do, but it will also help your children explore their creative side by having them practice drawing "a funny picture," "a picture that shows movement," "a picture that tells a story," or "a picture that is part of a larger scene."

Divergent Thinking
IMAGINATION DRAWING STATION

2. IMAGINATE SHAPES TASK

In this *Imaginate Shapes Task,* give your children a page filled with a series of the same shape (all circles, all squares, or all diamonds, etc.). Have them sketch objects or pictures that have that shape as a major part of the completed picture. For example, if the page is filled with circles, your children must imagine and draw as many objects as they can think of that would include a circle as the main part of the picture (glasses, smiley face, sun, wheel, etc.).

Here is an example done with a series of circles on a page:

Divergent Thinking
IMAGINATION DRAWING STATION

3. PICTURE CONSEQUENCES

Picture Consequences is a circle game in which a group of people cooperatively draw a person or creature. Historically, it was played by European artists commonly called Surrealists, beginning in the early 1920s.

In this process, a figure is drawn in portions, with the paper folded after each portion and passed to the next artist so that they cannot see the earlier portions. At the end, the paper is unfolded, and the completed figure is revealed.

This *Picture Consequences* activity can be played between yourself and your child, or between your children, or with your children and their play dates. Fold a piece of blank paper back and forth lengthwise into quarters. Give this piece of paper to the first child. Using crayons or a pencil have the child privately draw a head of some kind (human, animal or fantastical) in the first quarter, leaving a little bit of neck sticking down into the next quarter of the paper.

Have the child then fold over this first quarter of the paper so the drawing is covered but the neck is left showing into the next quarter.

The piece of paper is then passed on to the next player, who then adds a torso and arms (or wings or whatever) in the second quarter and then draws the tops of the legs down into the third quarter. Fold the paper again so that what has already been drawn continues to be hidden.

Have them pass the piece of paper on again, and this time legs (but not feet) are drawn in the third quarter. Fold and pass it on a final time, and finish with the feet in the last quarter.

The children can then unfold the paper together to discover a most amazing, zany creature.

The picture below was created by my daughter and one of my sons. They passed the paper back and forth to each other, covering their eyes when it was the other person's time to draw. Your child can do this Creative Mindflexor with friends, a playmate, siblings, or even with you. It's a fun way to explore collaborative imagination.

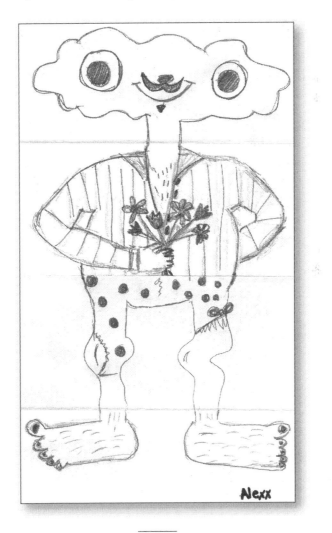

Originality
IMAGINATION DRAWING STATION

4. PICTURES TELL A STORY

Give your children a picture of a door, a window, a curtain, a building, an egg, etc. You can clip it out of a magazine, or print it off the computer, or draw it yourself. Ask your children to imagine and draw what they think is behind or inside the object in the picture. Their drawing should tell a story without words that is original and creative, full of imagery.

What's on the other side of this door?

Story Task

Alexx

Originality
TIME MACHINE SIMULATOR STIMULATOR

With the *Time Machine Simulator Stimulator* activity, you simulate time-machine travel in order to stimulate your children's creativity. In this Creative Mindflexor, you send your children either back or forward to a specific time, and you give them an activity to perform there. This activity would be one that, because of the time travel, would require your children to use their imagination in order to come up with a new way of performing the task. Depending on your children's age, you may have to give them additional information regarding what differences they may encounter traveling to certain time periods. For instance, tell your children you are sending them back in time before electricity was invented and ask them how they would cook a meal or how they would wake up at a specific time without an alarm clock. Or, send them forward in time and say, "In this time period, bicycles are a thing of the past," and have them describe what they see themselves riding on at the park.

There are many ways this Creative Mindflexor can be performed. You can have your children describe their answers to you, draw pictures, write a story, or even act them out. It is simple enough that you can play this at the dinner table in order to flex their creative minds. Have each person come up with a time period and activity for the family member next to them — working your way around the table as each person describes their answer and then comes up with a different *Time Machine Simulator Stimulator* for the person to their right.

You should encourage your children to be as innovative and detailed as they can be. And, remember, there are no wrong answers. It is a great way to encourage and help develop your children's imagination, innovation, and problem-solving abilities. If they are acting out their answers, you can help them get even more creative by supplying props for them to use: boxes, straws, hats, plastic cups — virtually anything you find lying around the house. It's especially fun for the kids if you let them actually create the time machine. It can be as simple as making it out of pillows and blankets draped over chairs, or, if you have a big box lying around, letting them draw on it with crayons or markers to make levers and lights.

When coming up with ideas for your "stimulators," think of the 1985 movie *Back to the Future* — a movie I recently had my children watch, which they loved. Send your kids back to the 1850s in the Wild West and tell them to turn their favorite video game into an actual physical activity that could have been played back then. Or, send them to the 1950s, and ask them how they would communicate with their friends without iPhones or texting. Or, send them to the Future and have them describe what their transportation to school would look like — maybe a Hoverboard? Ever since watching the movie, my youngest son keeps asking me when Marty McFly's Hoverboard (a skateboard without wheels that flies low to the ground) is going to be invented. Who knows, maybe some child is sitting around today, imagining up the idea as we speak, only to grow up one day and build it.

Originality
WHAT MIGHT HAVE BEEN

"Counterfactual thinking" is the technical term for looking at a situation that has already occurred and asking yourself, "What could have happened if some part of that scenario had been different?" According to research, thinking about "what might have been" can boost creativity.

A fun Creative Mindflexor is providing "What if" scenarios for your children and letting them describe to you, write a story, draw a picture, or even act out what that new scenario would look like. Some scenarios could be:

What might have happened if :

- Dinosaurs had never become extinct and instead became family pets?
- Dorothy, in *The Wizard of Oz*, never made it back to Kansas?
- Instead of the bald eagle becoming the national bird of the United States, it had been the turkey?
- Christopher Columbus had been a farmer?

After they have gotten the hang of responding to your scenarios, have them make up a few of their own.

Originality
PEOPLE WATCHING

Present your child with pictures from a magazine or images from the Internet. Have your child answer open-ended questions like: What are the people in the picture doing? What are the people saying? Where are they going? Why do you think they are laughing? What do you think they are looking at? Who do you think is living there? You can even do this by observing people with your children when you are at a restaurant or shopping in town, and have them try to come up with the most imaginative scenarios they can for the questions above.

Who do you think the people on this ship are?

Originality
MAKE IT BETTER

One way to help children to think more creatively is to ask them to change things to make them the way they would like them to be. For example:

- What would taste better if it was sweeter?

- What would be nicer if it was smaller?

- What would be more fun if it was faster?

- What would be better if it was quieter?

- What would be happier if it was bigger?

- What could be more exciting if it went backwards?

Fluency
BEDTIME RITUAL

"But, I'm not tired."

Sound familiar? Next time your child utters those words when you declare that it's bedtime, why not take advantage of the moment by using this bedtime Creative Mindflexor?

Part of encouraging creative thinking is helping children become fluent thinkers. Fluent thinkers have the ability to come up with many different ideas. You can help your children practice their fluent thinking by asking them to respond to questions that have many right answers. Incorporate these questions into the situations the child is experiencing — such as bedtime.

You can use this bedtime Creative Mindflexor to build your children's fluent thinking while they are lying in bed having trouble sleeping. Have them respond to open-ended questions. Ask them to think of everything that lights up in the night, all the people who work at night, all the things they'd like to do if they stayed up all night, or all the things a nocturnal animal might be doing during the night.

Instead of just counting sheep, you will be tuckering them out with all that thinking, all while preparing them to be a great idea-generating brainstormer one day. They might even fall asleep before finishing with their first list of ideas. Even better would be to make it a bedtime ritual to ensure you get some daily creativity practice in for them.

Fluency
LIST IT!

A good way to increase your children's creative fluency is by having them come up with lists of things that push their creative boundaries. Here are examples of some potential lists for them to work on:

- Generate many different uses for common items such as a pencil, ruler, or paper-towel tube.
- Generate synonyms for common words or phrases such as "good job."
- Generate many different ways to arrange the furniture in their bedroom (draw pictures).
- Generate names for a pet, sports team, or alternative titles to a book.
- Generate ideas for a birthday party.
- Generate questions about a given topic—if animals should be kept in a zoo, a current political race.
- Generate solutions to a recurring classroom problem. For example, the noise level is too high during work times, or students are feeling that they are not treated fairly during games at recess.
- Generate solutions to a regional or world issue such as poverty or global warming.
- Generate different ways they can organize the food items in the pantry.

Fluency
ALPHABET GAMES

Whenever my family goes to a restaurant, to keep my kids occupied while they wait for their food, I have them work on their Fluency of Thought by playing *Alphabet Games*. These are games that have my kids thinking up different items that start with the various letters of the alphabet. It's a good way to work on their fluency. Each person needs to come up with something from the chosen category for the letter that we are on. Game play passes to the right. We keep going until we have worked our way through from A to Z.

Here are a couple of category examples:

- Animals
- Foods
- Movies
- Songs
- Books
- Countries/Cities
- Girls'/Boys' Names
- Games
- Emotions
- Adjectives
- Transportation Modes

Elaboration
CREATURE CREATION

Ask your children to draw a creature from their imagination. Instruct them to add details such as horns, a beak, or feathers. Have them add on to their picture by drawing the creature's skin or feet or movement—the more elaborate, the better. If you like, you can make available for use any art materials you have on hand, such as feathers, pipe cleaners, glitter, or plastic eyes. In addition, have them write down words that describe these details either under the creature or in a list to the side of the creature. It's a good time to have your children explore new and interesting vocabulary as the ideas come up.

Alexx

Have your children use these elaboration strategies to help them further detail their creature:

- Have them describe the creature using their five senses: sight, touch, taste, sound, and smell.
- Have them think of similes and metaphors that compare their creature to something more concrete. When your children compare their creatures to a more familiar creature, it will feel like the imagined creature is more real. Does it roar like a lion? Does it slither like a snake? Challenge your children to come up with at least one sentence that compares their creature to another, well-known animal.
- Have them write down a line or two of what they think their creature would say if it could talk.

Elaboration
FIVE SENSES

To help your children become more aware of their environment and enhance their ability to perceive the world around them, have them try this exercise. First, find a stopwatch or a timer of some kind, and set it for five minutes. Wherever they are, have them take in the sights, sounds, and other sensations around them. Encourage them to look for patterns of color and light; view edges and angles of objects or walls; notice movement by people, objects, insects, and shadows; listen to sounds; pay attention to the tonal qualities of voices, the variations in any music they can detect, the rhythms of far-off noises such as dogs barking, rain hitting the roof or pavement, splashes in a bathtub, or the hum of traffic. Also have them note tactile sensations: The contours or texture of the surface on which they are sitting; the temperature and humidity of the air. Finally, encourage them to notice any faint odors — from food, flowers, or fuel. Continue this process until the timer sounds. If performed frequently, this exercise will condition your children to become more aware of what is new around them.

Elaboration
AS "BLANK" AS A "BLANK"

Using Metaphors/Similes and Synonyms is a way to elaborate on one's ideas. They can help expand your children's idea of looking at things. Use this activity with your children to get them used to using this skill and to help them understand the differences between them.

- **Metaphors** are used for connecting things indirectly. They are connections that are unusual or not an ordinary way of thinking: *A sea of troubles; the heart of a lion; raining cats and dogs.*
- **Similes** use "like" or "as" to illustrate the connection. *The boy was as agile as a monkey. The miner's face was like coal. The task was as easy as ABC. Dry as a raisin in the sun.*
- **A Synonym** is a word that means exactly the same or nearly the same as another word. If you ask people to list the ways to fasten two things together, they will probably come up with about eight. But if you look up the more specific synonyms of the verb "fasten" in a thesaurus, you will find at least sixty ways — buckle, clip, velcro, glue, tie, weld, sew, clamp, staple, etc.

Metaphor Activity

Share the following metaphors with your children, and have them explain to you what they mean. If they aren't sure of an answer, you can explain it to them. Then, see if they can come up with metaphors that they have heard of.

- No pain, no gain
- Break the ice
- Costs an arm and a leg
- Crying crocodile tears
- Step on it
- On the fly
- Surf the net
- Butterflies in your stomach

Simile Activity

In this activity, use this list to give your children the beginning of a simile and let them finish it. Remember, they can come up with any connection they want — it doesn't have to be the one that is the most familiar to them. Once they get the hang of it, see if they can come up with their own similes when they are trying to describe something.

- As big as a ...
- As brave as a ...
- As clean as a ...
- As cold as a ...
- As dry as ...
- As gentle as ...
- As hot as ...
- As mad as ...
- As old as ...
- As quick as ...
- As proud as ...
- As sharp as ...

- As slow as ...
- As strong as ...
- As wise as ...

Synonym Activity

This should be an ongoing activity that you do with your children. Whenever the opportunity arises — when your children inevitably ask you for another snack, a glass of water, dinner, their new pair of pants, or any of the other dozens of things children can ask from a parent each day — before handing over that item, ask your children to come up with at least two (if not more) other names that item can be called. This will get them in the habit of thinking up synonyms for items, which will help them with elaboration.

Elaboration
PARTY TIME!

Have your children plan a party for the family, friends, a pet, or a doll. Have them come up with a theme, and make a list of all the possible attributes of the party to which they can apply that theme.

- Invitations
- Décor
- Costumes
- Plates/Cups/Tablecloth
- Party Favors
- Activities

Then, have them break down those attributes and get as creative with designing their ideas as they can.

- Create their own invitations: Is there a riddle inside? Do they pop out? Is it a map?
- Décor: Go beyond streamers and balloons. Is there a pathway leading to the party room? What does the entrance look like? Is there a photo-op area?
- Costumes: Are there some helpers at the party that are dressed to represent the theme?
- Plates/Cups/Tablecloth: Is there an interesting centerpiece? Can a themed placemat be made?
- Party Favors: Don't buy the typical party-store-filled boxes. What is an interesting gift that would represent the theme, but not be expected?

- Activities: This is the area where your children should really test the boundaries of their imagination. Don't just settle for Pin the Tail on the Donkey!

Flexibility (and Convergent Thinking)
SOLVING SOCIAL SCENARIOS

Have your children consider a social scenario that bothers them. Have them set the timer for three minutes and write down as many ways to solve this problem as they can think of, without judging the quality of the solutions. Then, have them look over their list. Are there surprises? Then, they can sift out the silly ideas, holding on to the gems.

Some examples of social scenarios are:

* Another child bothers them on the playground.
* Their younger sibling is always "borrowing" their stuff.
* No one recycles in the lunchroom.

Have your children spend at least fifteen minutes weekly, or whenever they can, thinking in this "divergent" way about a practical problem in their lives.

Flexibility
WATER, WATER, EVERYWHERE

Take one concept/item, and ask your children many different open-ended questions about it across different "themes."

- What are some of the uses of water?

- What floats in water?

- How does water help us?

- Why is cold water cold?

- What always stays underwater?

- What are the different colors that water can be?

- What happens when someone gets dehydrated?

- How is a rainbow formed?

- Incorporate other concepts: fire, sand, clouds, ice, and erosion

Then get your children to come up with a topic of their own and break it down into various questions across various themes for you or another sibling or friend.

Flexibility
EMOTION COMMOTION

Give your children a picture of a boy who looks sad. Have them think of all the different things or reasons that could be making him look this way.

For example:

- He tripped and hurt himself.
- He's lost.
- Someone said something mean to him.
- He dropped his ice cream cone.
- He scored the last out in his baseball game.

Alexx

Convergent Thinking (and Flexibility)
RIDDLE ME THIS

Solving riddles is a great Creative Mindflexor to help your children first use "divergent thinking" by opening their minds to all the possible answers and then to use "convergent thinking" in choosing from all their generated, possible answers to determine what they think the best answer to the riddle is.

There are many types of riddles. Here are a few to use with your children to get you started. The answers are at the end of this post.

STORY RIDDLES:

A story riddle incorporates a story.

A clever boy wanted a candy bar but didn't have any money with him, so he tells the shopkeeper: "I know almost every song that has ever been written."

The shopkeeper laughs at this, but the boy says, "I am willing to bet you a candy bar that I can sing a song that you have heard of with the woman's name of your choice in it."

"Deal," says the shopkeeper. "How about my mother's name, 'Felicity Jane Ashley'?"

So the boy sang and earned himself a free candy bar.

What song did he sing?

REBUS PUZZLES:

Rebus Puzzles are little pictures, often made with letters and words, which cryptically represent a word, phrase, or saying.

Can you guess what each of these three word pictures are trying to say?

1. TRY   STAND
            2

2. IN   VADERS

3. M CE

    M CE

    M CE

ASSOCIATED WORD PUZZLES:

In an associated word puzzle, a list of words is given. To solve the puzzle, think of a single word that goes with each to form a compound word (or word pair that functions as a compound word).

Can you think of a word associated with all three of these words, in each of these two puzzles?

1. Swiss, cottage, cake

2. motion, poke, down

MATH PUZZLES:

A math puzzle involves using math or logic to guess the answer.

A bat and a ball cost $1.10. The bat costs $1.00 more than the ball. How much does the ball cost?

WHO/WHAT AM I PUZZLES:

These puzzles involve a riddle whose answer is either a person, place, or thing.

1. What can you catch but not throw?

2. What gets wetter and wetter the more it dries?

3. What goes around the world but stays in a corner?

4. I have an eye, but cannot see. I am stronger and faster than any man alive, but have no limbs. Who am I?

5. I am a five-letter word that is under you. If you remove my first letter, then I am over you. If you remove my first and second letters, then I am all around you. What am I?

ANSWERS:

Story Puzzle: He sang "Happy Birthday", of course! **Rebus Puzzle:** 1. Try to understand; 2. Space Invaders; 3. Three blind mice (Three mice without "eyes"). **Associated Word Puzzle:** 1. Cheese; 2. Slow. **Math Puzzle:** The ball costs 5 cents. One dollar more than 5 cents is $1.05, the sum of which is $1.10. **Who/What Am I Puzzles:** 1. a cold; 2. a towel; 3. a stamp; 4. a hurricane; 5. A chair.

YOUR OWN RIDDLES

It's not only fun to answer riddles, but it's also fun to make up your own. You can help your children come up with their own riddles. The Who/What Am I? riddles are the easiest to start with — just follow these three steps:

1. Think of what you want the answer to be.

2. Think of things your answer does and what they look like.

3. Write a draft of your riddle, and then rewrite it.

Good luck — and get creative!

CREATIVE MINDFLEXORS FOR BRAINSTORMING TECHNIQUES

Mind Mapping

As discussed earlier, a Mind Map is a diagram used to visually outline a brainstorming session. One creates a mind map around the problem he or she is trying to solve or the issue he or she is addressing, placed in a circle in the center. One draws lines off of that circle and labels those lines with associated ideas, words, and concepts. In order for your children to practice this technique, try giving them a family decision to mind map. For instance, for "Where should we go on vacation?" lines off of that center could be: possible climates (warm, cold), possible modes of transportation to take to get there (plane, car, train), possible types of activities (sightseeing, relaxation, active).

Possible family decisions:

1. Where should we go on vacation?
2. What should we do this weekend?
3. What movie should we watch?
4. Where should we go out to eat?
5. What should we make the spare bedroom into?

Free Association

The process of free association is to get one to go beyond a topic and explore how things are associated *(or related)* in one's mind. Play a game with your children or between siblings in which you start off with a word, and the next person has to say the first word that comes to mind when they hear that word. Then, you say a word that you think of when you hear the word your child came up with — keep going.

Parent: Apple
Child: Red
Parent: Car
Child: Fast
Parent: Cheetah
Child: Cat
Parent: Pet
Child: Dog
Parent: Leash
Child: Walk
Parent: Feet
Child: Toes
Parent: Little Piggies
Child: Wolf
Parent: Howl
Child: Moon
Parent: Harvest
Child: Farm
Parent: Apple

Attribute Analysis

Attribute Analysis is a technique used to investigate and improve tangible things. Have your children think of a particular item, and then list all the attributes of that item that they can think of. List parts, functions, features, bonuses, and every characteristic of the item. Then, you can start asking questions that could lead to ways in which the item could be improved, combined with another thing, simplified, added to, or phased out of use.

Ex. *Backpack*

Parts: Pack, Straps, Pockets, Zippers
Function: Carry Books, Carry Coats, Carry Lunch
Features: Style, Size, Material
Improve: Add Cooling System to keep you cool on hot days; add pockets designed to better distribute the weight
Combined: Jet Pack, Pop-up Umbrella, a Stand
Simplified: Push-button strap adjustments
Phased out: One of the straps, since most kids wear it over just one shoulder

Empathy Design

Empathic design is a process that involves observation, data collection and analysis, and prototyping. It is identified as a way to uncover people's unspoken latent needs and then address them through design — by responding to real, but unexpressed and unmet, needs.

Give your children or have them think of a product or an item or an experience that they think they could improve on. One example is a particular video game. Have them watch another person play the game and notate where in the game the person grimaces or says something that shows they are frustrated or upset. Then, have them review that particular part of the video game and brainstorm on ideas that would improve the game and alleviate the player's frustration at that particular point in the game.

SCAMPER

Each of the letters in the acronym SCAMPER stands for a stage in the process of trying to look at and dissect your problem/issue in different ways in order to spur more creative ideas.

Substitute
Combine
Adapt
Modify
Put to other uses
Eliminate or Elaborate
Rearrange

Have your children find something around the house that doesn't work well: A leaky faucet, a door that gets stuck, a room that's not well-insulated, a picture frame that is broken, a chair that is wobbly, etc.

Using the "SCAMPER" technique, have your children work out ways to either fix the item/situation or find another use for the item.

Chapter Seventeen
Final Thoughts

In order to combat this Creativity Crisis, we all have to do our part. As parents, we need to act as supporters, coaches, facilitators, and models of creativity for our children. We need to make sure we are encouraging creativity by:

- asking open-ended questions
- tolerating ambiguity
- modeling creative thinking and behavior
- encouraging experimentation and persistence
- praising our children when they provide unexpected answers

It's also important to put the emphasis on the creative "process," rather than to judge the quality of your child's "products" or "solutions." Each child's creative abilities should be related to his/her personal stage of development. Your child's work may be original for that particular child and/or in relation to children in their age group.

Also, keep in mind that, although some children already see themselves as creative and will be self-motivated to participate in the outlined activities, others may need help, encouragement, and skill development in order to engage in creative activity. People are creative because they choose to be, so finding out about and encouraging a child's own interests is an important starting point. The more you can make the activity fun for them, the more apt they will be to participate.

You can play a crucial role in nurturing this important life-skill. While everyone else is just talking about the free-fall of children's creativity, you can be taking action and making certain your child doesn't end up as part of that statistic.

By providing a creative environment for your children to grow up in, making sure you put a value on creativity enhancement so that you allow time for your children to work on it, and keeping creativity training fun and positive for them, you are helping to mold your children into better problem solvers, idea generators, and innovators. You are helping them build a skill that will position them to be more successful in life in general. And, for many children, they aren't receiving this training from anywhere or from anyone else. The success of the future of our children, our economy, and our country may rely on the diligence of parents, now more than ever.

Endnotes

[1] *Understanding Creativity: The Interplay of Biological, Psychological and Social Factors*, Dacey and Lennon, 1998

[2] *American Scientist*, Nicholas Turiano, June 2012

[3] *Fast Company*, Austin Carr, May 2010

[4] *The Relevance of Creativity in Education*, Dr. Rosa Aurora Chavez-Eakle, 2010

[5] *Creative Intelligence*, Bruce Nussbaum, 2013

[6] *Creativity and Education: Why It Matters*, Adobe, 2012

[7] *All I Really Need to Know (About Creative Thinking) I Learned (By Studying How Children Learn) in Kindergarten*, Mitchel Resnick, 2007

[8] *Barriers to Creativity in Education*, Adobe, 2013

[9] *Generation M2: Media in the Lives of 8- to 18-year-olds*, Kaiser Family Foundation, January 2010

[10] *Growing Up Creative: Nurturing a Lifetime of Creativity*, Teresa Amabile, 1992

[11] *Things You Didn't Know About Yourself: 12 Facts About Your Creativity*, Smart Decisions, 2014

[12] *Why It's Dangerous to Label People*, Psychology Today, Adam Alter, 2010

[13] *The Structural Relationships of Parenting Style, Creative Personality, and Loneliness*, S. Lim and J. Smith, 2008

[14] *Creative Problem Solving for Teachers*, Donald Treffinger, 1984

[15] *Enhancing Creativity Through Play: A Discussion of Parental and Environmental Factors*, Ellermeyer, 1993

[16] *Why Boredom is Good for Your Child*, Aha! Parenting, Dr. Laura Markham, 2014

[17] *The Neuroscience of Imagination*, Christopher Bergland, 2012

[18] *It's Not 'Mess.' It's Creativity.* NY Times, Kathleen D. Vohs, 2013

[19] *Travel Abroad? A way to increase creativity?* Ernest Gurman, 1989

About the Author

Jackie McCarthy founded *Raise Creative Kidz* in an effort to combat the Creativity Crisis that is currently afflicting our children. By providing educational talks, informative websites, and creativity-training tools, Jackie is helping parents, communities, and schools to cultivate and nourish children's creative intelligence. Jackie's background as a former marketing executive for a Fortune 500 company included developing innovative marketing campaigns based on social and psychological research. She uses similar techniques in her development of fun, creative-thinking-enhancement activities and hands-on *Creative Mindflexors*® tools. For additional activity ideas, current creativity research, and a link to purchase her *Creative Mindflexors*® tools, please view *www.RaiseCreativeKidz.com*. To inquire about hiring her for speaking engagements, Jackie can be contacted at *Jackie@RaiseCreativeKidz.com*.

20478764R00083

Made in the USA
Lexington, KY
05 December 2018